PRAY **FIRST** CHALLENGE

BOOKS BY ANDREW F CARTER

The Privilege of Prayer

Pray First Challenge

PRAY
FIRST
CHALLENGE

60 Devotions to Grow in Faith, Family,
Fitness, Finances, and Future

ANDREW F CARTER

Chosen
a division of Baker Publishing Group
Minneapolis, Minnesota

© 2024 by Andrew F Carter

Published by Chosen Books
Minneapolis, Minnesota
ChosenBooks.com

Chosen Books is a division of
Baker Publishing Group, Grand Rapids, Michigan

Printed in China

Library of Congress Cataloging-in-Publication Data
Names: Carter, Andrew Formby, author.
Title: Pray first challenge : 60 devotions to grow in faith, family, fitness, finances, and future / Andrew F. Carter.
Description: Minneapolis, Minnesota : Chosen Books, a division of Baker Publishing Group, [2024]
Identifiers: LCCN 2024000644 | ISBN 9780800763527 (cloth) | ISBN 9781493442515 (e-book)
Subjects: LCSH: Prayers--Christianity. | Life cycle, Human--Religious aspects—Christianity.
Classification: LCC BV225 .C47 2024 | DDC 242—dc23/eng/20240216
LC record available at https://lccn.loc.gov/2024000644

Unless otherwise indicated, Scriptures are taken from the Holy Bible, New International Version®, NIV®. Copyright © 1973, 1978, 1984, 2011 by Biblica, Inc.® Used by permission of Zondervan. All rights reserved worldwide. www.zondervan.com. The "NIV" and "New International Version" are trademarks registered in the United States Patent and Trademark Office by Biblica, Inc.®

Cover design by David Carlson, Studio Gearbox

Published in association with The Bindery Agency, www.TheBindery Agency.com.

Baker Publishing Group publications use paper produced from sustainable forestry practices and postconsumer waste whenever possible.

24 25 26 27 28 29 30   7 6 5 4 3 2 1

CONTENTS ▶

To my incredible family of followers, your unwavering support, likes, comments, and shares have been the fuel for my creative fire. Your enthusiasm for my work has inspired me to push boundaries, explore new ideas, and strive for excellence with every post.

Through your virtual presence, you've become a part of my journey as an author, offering encouragement, feedback, and camaraderie. Your engagement has transformed this online community into a family.

Thank you for believing in me, for joining me on this adventure, and for being the heartbeat of my digital world. This book is dedicated to each one of you, with deepest gratitude and boundless appreciation.

With love,
Andrew F Carter

INTRODUCTION

Welcome to the *Pray First Challenge* devotional, a sixty-day journey designed for Christians who are seeking a deeper connection with God through the transformative power of prayer.

Within these pages lies an invitation to dive into the rich tapestry of devotion and prayer. Consistent daily prayer is a practice that anchors faith, fosters communion with God, and ignites spiritual growth. You will be encouraged to immerse yourself in Scripture, to make observations, to consider applications, and to join in heartfelt prayers crafted to enrich your walk with God.

Each day has a Scripture passage that aligns with a personal experience or thought God has walked with me through. I've added prayers that I've prayed during some of the toughest times in my life and, as a result, have witnessed the hand of God move mountains to make a way I previously hadn't been able to see.

My passion for consistent prayer is what led me to write this devotional. The five areas I talk about are some of the most challenging aspects of our daily lives—*Faith, Family, Fitness, Finances, and Future*. Each area has a unique pain point to which the Bible speaks and guides us. These also represent some of the aspects of our lives in which it is most difficult for us to admit that we may be struggling. No one wants to admit they lack faith, their family is in shambles, their finances are in disarray, their fitness is nonexistent, or they have no hope for the future. Within these pages, I share the same Scripture verses and stories that have comforted me in the past.

My hope is that the time spent in each daily devotion will draw you closer to the heart of God. I encourage you to purchase a journal to write down what God says to you and to process what you're reading. This devotional serves as your companion on the path toward a more intimate relationship with the Creator, guiding you to discover the profound joy and peace found in a life devoted to prayerful communion with the Almighty. If God can do it for me, He can most certainly do it for you.

1

THEY FOLLOW YOUR LEAD

"But as for me and my household, we will serve the LORD."

Joshua 24:15

We are presented with countless choices every day. Some are seemingly inconsequential, while others are profoundly significant. Among the sea of choices, the decision to follow the Lord is the most crucial one we will ever make. This verse reminds us that our choices should reflect our commitment to God.

The world may tempt us with its fleeting pleasures, its idols, and its distractions, just as it did the Israelites in Joshua's time. We may be enticed to follow the crowd, to go after worldly pursuits, or to conform to the values of the culture around us. In the face of these temptations, however, Joshua's words serve as an unwavering beacon of faith, guiding us to choose the Lord above all else.

As we navigate the problems of life, let us take note and follow suit. Day after day, we should choose to serve the Lord with all our heart, to make Him the compass that guides our decisions, and to lead our households by example. Our commitment to follow God's lead will not only have an impact on our lives but also create a legacy of faith for those who come after us.

Remember that little eyes of the children around you are watching, and they will mimic what they see. Kids will follow what you do over what you say. Let this proclamation be etched in your heart and be a constant reminder of your devotion to the One true God who lovingly leads you on the path of righteousness and everlasting joy. Be mindful of how you live, because how you live matters.

> *Father God,* help me to live a life that brings glory and honor to Your name. Give me the direction and discernment to make choices that keep me in alignment with Your will, and give me the peace of knowing that a life spent walking with You is a life well spent. In the sea of

*things competing for my attention, I choose You.
In Jesus' name, amen.*

What is one specific action you feel called to make today? What can you do to lead your family to follow and serve the Lord?

2

THE ESSENCE OF FAITH

Now faith is confidence in what we hope for and assurance about what we do not see.

Hebrews 11:1

Faith can be a scary concept. Taking a step forward without knowing where that step is going to lead takes trust. You must trust the One who is calling you to take that step. That's not easy, especially if you've ever experienced hurt, pain, disappointment, or betrayal, which I assume you have.

The beautiful thing about faith in God is that He's good. Let that sink in for just a moment. He's good, faithful, loving, kind, compassionate, merciful, and righteous. He loves you! He wants what's best for you. It doesn't always feel like it, but you can be certain that He sees the bigger picture and knows exactly where He's leading you.

We can have confidence in God. We may have been let down by people, but He will never let us down. He's not like us. He doesn't change His mind about things a million different times. He's the same yesterday, today, and forever (see Hebrews 13:8). He's already made up His mind about you and chosen you to know Him. That's good news! We can live with boldness knowing that where He leads, He'll provide and fully equip us for the journey.

Clearly, living a life of faith won't always be easy, nor will it always make sense. Honestly, most of the time it's challenging and makes no sense at all. But we can rely on God because we know who He is. We can boldly take steps forward into the unknown because of the One who holds our hand. We can hold tight with confidence and hope, assured that He is with us no matter how difficult things appear.

What steps of faith is God asking you to take in this season of life? What are your hang-ups? What are your fears? What's stopping you from trusting the One who is calling you into the unknown?

Father God, help me to be more trusting. I sometimes allow fear of the unknown to stop me from

stepping forward. Teach me to walk with bold-
ness and the assurance that You'll never leave me
nor forsake me. My hope is in You, and I know
You'll never let me down. In Jesus' name, amen.

Speak the prayer above out loud, and then continue with bold requests of God made in faith, trusting in His goodness.

3

TEMPLE OF THE SPIRIT

Do you not know that your bodies are temples of the Holy Spirit, who is in you, whom you have received from God? You are not your own; you were bought at a price. Therefore honor God with your bodies.

1 Corinthians 6:19–20

One of the things we overlook most in the body of Christ is our health. If you've been to any church conferences, gatherings, potlucks, celebrations, or groups, you've probably noticed that the food served isn't usually healthful. These events often offer soda, pizza, doughnuts, and other foods with little to no nutritional value. We scream from the rooftops about sin and living holy lives but forget that gluttony and self-control are things we should be paying attention to as well.

When we talk about honoring our bodies, we focus on the idea of being pure from sexual immorality, avoiding excessive alcohol, or not marking our bodies with tattoos. Yet we turn a blind eye to preventable diseases caused by overeating and laziness. We have to do better. Our bodies are temples for the Holy Spirit. We should be stewarding them better.

Health and fitness shouldn't consume our lives, but shouldn't be afterthoughts, either. We need to be intentional about how we feed, move, hydrate, and rest our bodies. This is part of keeping ourselves fit for God's service. If God calls you on a mission trip to evangelize to others in a remote part of the world, you have to be physically ready. If God calls you to participate in twelve outreaches in a row, you have to be physically ready. If God calls you to preach five sermons in a day, you have to be physically ready. You must be on call and ready for service when God opens doors.

You have been bought with a price. Are you honoring and caring for the body God gave you? Are you stewarding it well? Or are there some areas of improvement that need attending to?

Father God, help me to steward my body better. Give me the desire and tools needed to make improvements in my health. Teach me to make decisions and choices with my body that honor You and glorify Your name. I want to be fit for service. Please ignite a passion in me that leads to lasting life change in my physical well-being. In Jesus' name, amen.

Write in your journal two areas of physical fitness you desire to implement to be a temple of the Holy Spirit that is ready for what He has next for you. How can you act on one of them today?

4

GOD'S PROVISION

And my God will meet all your needs according to the riches of his glory in Christ Jesus.

Philippians 4:19

Within the context of our relationship with God, the word *provision* can mean many things. It usually refers to the act of supplying goods, services, resources, or support. Where God guides, He provides. If God calls you to it, He'll bring you through it.

We already have everything we need to fulfill the plan, purpose, and will of God. This is a challenging concept because we always feel as though something is missing, and we constantly want more. People are largely unsatisfied and live as if God owes them something. The truth is that our needs are fully met in Jesus.

Let me break this down. If you woke up today, you are blessed. You hopefully have the next twenty-four hours to live out God's plan. Yesterday is gone and can't be changed, and tomorrow isn't here yet. So, for today, God has a plan for you to accomplish. This could include a multitude of things. He might lead you to evangelize on a street corner, check on a friend, rest, save a kitten from a tree, write a Christian book, take care of your family, read your devotions, or serve a neighbor. The plans God has for you in a single day are endless.

For the next twenty-four hours, you already have or will have all the things you need to accomplish this purpose. Unfortunately, we don't see life this way. We spend most of our days trying to escape the present moment through daydreaming, regretting things in our past, or future tripping, which means worrying and being anxious about things that might happen in the future. We miss the provision for today by focusing on the concerns of tomorrow.

As the body of Christ, we need to get to the place where we truly live for God, not simply live for what He can do for us. Use today to reflect on areas where you may be overlooking the blessings and provisions that are right in front of you.

Lord God Almighty, help me to see Your provision each day. Teach me to be fully present in the tasks for the day that You've laid out. Show me how You meet all of my needs in Jesus. I believe and trust that all the things I need to live for You are already in my possession. I pray this in Jesus' name, amen.

Make a list in your journal of the many ways God has provided for you in the past. List as many as you can. Express gratitude for those things, and then anticipate how He will meet your present needs.

5

GOD'S PLANS FOR YOUR LIFE

"For I know the plans I have for you," declares the
LORD, "plans to prosper you and not to harm you,
plans to give you hope and a future."

Jeremiah 29:11

The plans we have for our lives often pale in comparison to what God made us for. A lot of our goals are derived from what we've been exposed to. We see others living lives that we find attractive and allow them to influence what we pursue. This isn't bad or wrong, it just shows how easily we can be influenced.

Think back to when you were a kid. You might have wanted to do something with your life that was influenced by a teacher, an athlete, an entertainer, a parent, or a family member. We're influenced by what we're exposed to. Some of the dreams and directions we pursue are because God planted those desires in our hearts. Other times, we are driven by curiosity and the desire to create our own plans.

It is important that we go to the Creator for our plans rather than inviting Him in to bless the ones we make. We often go after our own dreams, visions, and goals, asking God to bless them without asking if we're even supposed to be pursuing them. We should want God's plan for our life more than we want our own. We don't want to go where God isn't leading. We don't want to walk through a door God didn't open.

Where God guides, He provides. And that provision is sweet, it's safe, and it's solid. It's not always easy, and it might come with obstacles. But we have a peace that accompanies His provision knowing that He's with us.

Heavenly Father, lead me by the hand, and don't let go. I tend to wander off after my own desires, so bring me back into step with You. Show me how to keep my eyes on where You're leading me in the future. Close any doors that You didn't open and take away any opportunities that are meant to distract. I want what You want for me. In Jesus' name, amen.

What plans are you making without including God? Are you going places without His guidance? Take time today to present your plans to the Lord and ask Him if they line up with His plans. If they don't, make the changes necessary to get back into alignment with where He's going.

6

LAYING A
FOUNDATION

*Start children off on the way they should go, and
even when they are old they will not turn from it.*

Proverbs 22:6

Parenting is unique and a huge responsibility. It is the
art of molding hearts and minds and a journey of
nurturing souls. As parents, we are entrusted with stewarding the character and values of the next generation.

Proverbs 22:6 provides us with a guiding light in this
sacred endeavor. It urges us to start children off on the
way they should go by laying a strong foundation from
the very beginning. Just as a building's stability depends
on a solid foundation, so does a child's future. It depends
on the principles and values instilled in their upbringing.

As parents, we are not babysitters; we are stewards of future leaders. The choices we make, the values we impart, and the example we set influence the paths our children will take.

Laying a foundation means teaching our children biblical values such as love, kindness, empathy, and integrity. It involves nurturing their spiritual growth, helping them develop a moral compass, and instilling in them a hunger for truth and righteousness. It also means fostering their unique gifts and talents and empowering them to explore their God-given potential.

This verse helps remind us that we need to guide our children in the way they should go. The hope is that they will carry those values and lessons with them throughout life. Even when they are old, we believe that the foundation we've laid will remain solid, guiding them in their choices and influencing their character.

Parenting is a journey filled with challenges and joys, but it is also a privilege. Let us embrace this role with intentionality and prayer, seeking divine wisdom to raise children who walk in the ways of the Lord. May we lay a foundation that not only withstands the storms of life but also becomes a beacon of light for generations to come.

Lord God, we thank You for the gift of parenthood. You have shown us how to love and lead by example. Give us the strength and direction to lay a solid foundation in our kids' lives so that when they are grown and on their own, they won't abandon their faith. Engrain in their hearts a passion and zeal for the heavenly things that lead them back to You. In Jesus' name, amen.

Encourage and empower a gift or talent you see in your children, grandchildren, or the children with whom you have influence. Find a practical way to help them continue to explore their God-given potential.

7

FAITH COMES BY HEARING

Consequently, faith comes from hearing the message, and the message is heard through the word about Christ.

Romans 10:17

as your faith ever been a little shaky? Have you ever struggled with trying to understand what God is doing in your life? Have you ever questioned where God is leading you? Like most people, the answer is probably a resounding yes! In fact, you might have done all three in the last week.

The truth is that life can be tricky. We don't have all the answers, and God's plan isn't always clear. So, why do some people appear as if they have it all figured out?

I would say it's because they have a solid foundation of faith.

As Scripture suggests, faith comes from hearing the message, and the message is found in God's Word. The confidence you see in followers of Jesus who appear to have it all together comes from the fact they're grounded and rooted in the Word. Their lives are built on a firm foundation to the point that no matter what lies ahead, their faith doesn't waver. Their faith is built on Jesus.

Our faith can be built by knowing who we are, knowing who God is, and knowing whose we are. We know these things from reading and believing the truths found in the Word of God. Charles Spurgeon said, "A Bible that's falling apart usually belongs to a person that isn't."* The person who spends time devoted to the Word isn't easily moved because their faith is anchored in Christ.

Are you spending regular time studying the Word of God? When your faith wavers, what do you do? Are you building your life on solid ground or sinking sand? We make time for the things that are important to us, so how important is the strengthening of your faith?

*Bear Clifton, "A Bible That's Falling Apart Usually Belongs to a Person Who's Not," June 7th, 2019, *TrainYourselfMinistry.com*, https://www.trainyourselfministry.com/a-bible-thats-falling-apart-usually-belongs-to-someone-whos-not/#:~:text=You%20gotta%20walk%20before%20you,of%20your%20Bible%20one%20day.

Lord, my faith is in You. Although I allow it to waver, I know that You are good and faithful. Build me up in You. Ignite a fire and passion for Your Word deep inside my bones. Help me to hunger and thirst for Your truth that is only satisfied by time spent in Your presence. Grow in me the discipline needed to make more time for You. In Jesus' name, amen.

Amidst life's busyness, carve out a moment for silent reflection. Find one Scripture verse that strengthens your faith and read it aloud a few times. Ask the Holy Spirit to ground you in its truth.

8

RENEWAL IN THE LORD

But those who hope in the LORD will renew their strength. They will soar on wings like eagles; they will run and not grow weary, they will walk and not be faint.

Isaiah 40:31

If we allow it, life can become a grind. God didn't save us to use and abuse us to the point that we burn out. Unfortunately, that's how a lot of Christians live their lives. I've been guilty of it!

When I first started in ministry and planted our church, I did a live daily Bible study on social media for 372 days straight. Talk about a grind. I didn't miss a single day for over a year. Hundreds of people came to Christ, lives were changed, and people were delivered. It was an amazing season. But at the end of that season, I was burnt out and exhausted.

I went on a ten-day trip to Israel and got some much-needed rest. As I spent time in reflection, I felt the gentle conviction that I needed to slow down. God allowed me to grind it out for a time, but I realized that exhaustion was never His goal or intention for me. What drove me was the opinion of others, the applause I received, the fear of failure, and the rush of doing something good for God.

We can accomplish some good things in our own strength. They can be fruitful and have an impact, but operating on our own is never sustainable. It's not a matter of *if* you'll burn out, it's a matter of *when*. I found that God used my stubbornness for His glory, but I also found that if I acted, ministered, and served in His strength rather than my own, the effort would be sustainable.

I started to implement a different rhythm by building in a lot more rest. I took time to recover, doing things that filled my cup, so that I could operate in His strength and make changes as the Spirit led. The impact I had quadrupled, and the Bible studies became more insightful. By allowing God to lead, more lives were changed. Put your hope and trust in Him. His way is better than ours.

Dear Lord, Your ways are better than mine. Forgive me for taking matters into my own hands, and help me to surrender total control to You. Teach me to follow Your lead and to take instruction from the Spirit. Show me the areas where I'm likely to burn out, and renew my strength in You. In Jesus' name, amen.

Look at your activities over the past two months. How much are you doing in your own strength? What activities do you need to eliminate? Ask a mentor or trusted friend how he or she gets renewed and consider how to apply some of those insights to your life.

9

HONORING GOD WITH YOUR WEALTH

Honor the LORD with your wealth, with the firstfruits of all your crops; then your barns will be filled to overflowing, and your vats will brim over with new wine.

Proverbs 3:9–10

God deserves more than just our leftovers. Yet for some reason, that's what many of us give Him. Our leftover time, our leftover energy, and our leftover resources. And when we don't have anything left over, He gets nothing from us.

We should be honoring God with the best of what we have. Giving generously is a way we can express and proclaim that we have faith in the One who supplies all our needs. We're financially giving back to the One who gives to us. It's our heartfelt way of demonstrating the trust we have in Him by laying down our first and best, knowing that we'll be taken care of.

I've wrestled with this principle for years because of how I grew up. My family was extremely impoverished, and it never seemed as though we had enough money. This instilled in me a scarcity mindset, which is the belief that resources, opportunities, and good things in life are in short supply. When you have a scarcity mindset, you tend to focus on what you lack, constantly worry about not having enough, and often approach life with a sense of fear or competition. With this mindset, I never felt as if I had enough for myself, let alone God.

When I came to Christ and was given a new life, I was introduced to the concept of generosity and giving. It radically changed my perspective. Scripture verse after verse teaches us about God's love and provision. As His children, we are well taken care of and fully provided for. Giving money back to God isn't an obligation but a privilege that allows us to show Him who we deem to be the Lord of our life.

How do you view generosity and giving? Do you wrestle with a scarcity mindset? Do you think that giving tithes and offerings to God is a waste? Or if you give offerings to God's Kingdom, do you fear there won't be anything left for you? What changes can you make to be more intentional with how you honor God in this area?

Heavenly Father, help me to step out in faith and better honor You with the firstfruits of what I earn. Give me a heart that's blessed by generosity and that is eager to give back to You what's truly Yours. Break the hold that money has on my life and show me how to glorify Your name with things You've allowed me to steward. In Jesus' name, amen.

Intentionally perform an act of kindness and reflect Christ's love today by being generous. Then consider how you can align your giving to exemplify the Christian value of generosity.

10

FEAR NOT, HE'S WITH YOU

"So do not fear, for I am with you; do not be dismayed, for I am your God. I will strengthen you and help you; I will uphold you with my righteous right hand."

Isaiah 41:10

God didn't give us a spirit of fear. The enemy loves to use fear as a primary tactic to keep us from experiencing the fullness of God. By using lies and deception, he tries to convince us that God has left us, that He doesn't hear us, and that He no longer cares about us. These are all false accusations against the true nature and character of God. This is why it's important to know what the Word says about Him. If you fail to know Him, you will settle for a false representation of who He is.

When fear is attached to something God is calling you to do, recognize that the enemy is trying to stop you. Fear in the body produces three natural reactions: fight, flight, or freeze. When faced with fear, we either stand our ground and charge forward, we turn tail and flee as fast as we can, or we freeze and become motionless, neither moving forward nor backward. The enemy doesn't want you to fight. He wants to scare you off or get you to stop in your tracks. He doesn't want you to pursue the plan and purpose God has for your life.

When you know who your enemy is and how he operates, you can better prepare yourself for his attacks and tactics. When you know who your Father is, you can move with the authority, strength, and power you've been given in Christ. When you don't stand on the truth of God's Word, you're bound to fall for anything.

When fear becomes louder than faith, recognize that the enemy is trying to distract you and cause you to miss something God is doing. So, in the presence of fear, pay attention to God and listen closely to what He's saying. Run to the Word so that you don't slip into a spiral of fear and worry.

When you're faced with fear, where do you look for peace?

God, help me to keep my faith louder than my fears. Teach me to run to You when things feel out of control. Strengthen me, uphold me, and help me with Your righteous hand. Bind the enemy and remind me that although the weapons may form, they will not prosper. I stand on Your truth so that I won't fall for the lies. In Jesus' name, amen.

What fear has become louder than your faith? Declare out loud Isaiah 41:10 (see above) and continue to stand upon this truth until it overcomes fear.

11

LEAD WITH LOVE

Above all, love each other deeply, because love covers over a multitude of sins. Offer hospitality to one another without grumbling.

1 Peter 4:8-9

In a world filled with division, strife, and self-centeredness, this verse reminds us of our calling as followers of Jesus: lead with love. Unfortunately, this truth is not always seen in the Church.

Love is not merely an option or a nice thought; it is the cornerstone of our faith and the essence of God's character. We are called to love unconditionally and without boundaries, to love in a way that mirrors God's overwhelming love for us. In many instances, the world does a better job at loving people than Christians do.

God's love has power. It can heal wounds, bridge gaps, and cover over a multitude of sins. When we choose to love deeply, we extend grace, mercy, and forgiveness to others, just as God has extended it to us. Love doesn't excuse wrongdoing but seeks to reconcile and restore.

And what about hospitality? True hospitality isn't about superficial gestures or perfect settings. It is about the state of our heart. It's about serving others with joy even when inconvenienced. It's about creating a space where people feel valued, worthy, accepted, and loved.

When we lead with love and offer hospitality without grumbling, we embody the essence of Christ's ministry on earth. Jesus welcomed sinners, ate with outcasts, and showed compassion to the hurting. His love was radical, transformative, and sacrificial.

As we journey through life, let us remember these words from Peter. Through acts of love, we not only draw nearer to God but also become torch bearers of His love in a world that desperately needs it. Lead with love and watch as it transforms your life and the lives of those around you.

Lord, as You look down at us as the body and see our self-inflicted wounds, help us. Help us lead with love and use the same measure of grace toward others that was extended to us. Teach us to operate out of selflessness and generosity without complaining. Transform and soften our hearts and give us the capacity to love deeper. In Jesus' name, amen.

What is one way you can prioritize love today and cultivate a spirit of genuine hospitality?

12

BELIEVE AND DON'T DOUBT

But when you ask, you must believe and not doubt, because the one who doubts is like a wave of the sea, blown and tossed by the wind.

James 1:6

The world we live in fosters widespread skepticism. Promises of quick fixes, get-rich-quick schemes, and recipes for overnight success have let a lot of people down. Many of us live by the creed that anything with potential is too good to be true. And in many cases, we're right.

When it comes to faith, however, we must operate in a manner that doesn't come naturally. To believe without doubting can be hard! Our minds are filled with alternate endings, questions, and potential outcomes. We're constantly calculating the risks, the potential returns, and our options. Our decision making and willingness to step out in faith is like a wild rollercoaster ride. It can be nauseating.

Why does God ask us to believe and not doubt knowing the world in which we live? It's because He wants us to know who He is. He is trustworthy. He is faithful. He is reliable. He is all the things the world can never be. Because of this, we can trust Him in ways in which we could never trust the world.

Our doubt stems from the ways we've been let down and disappointed by people. We can't bring that disappointment into our relationship with God. If we find ourselves let down or disappointed with God, it's not because He fell short, it's because our expectations or desires weren't met. That's on us, and it's our responsibility to reflect and see where we may have misunderstood His character or plan.

Doubt will kill 100 percent of your dreams. It will stop you in your tracks, halt forward progress, and prevent you from reaching your goals. When you find yourself wrestling with doubt, go back to the place of promise.

Dear Lord, please forgive my unbelief. I've allowed my fears to become louder than my faith.

Teach me to take my doubts to You and remind me of who You are. Help me to trust You. You are the author and finisher of my faith, and what You want for me is for Your good and Your glory. In Jesus' name, amen.

Answer the following questions in your journal. What are you doubting? Who are you doubting? Is this an obstacle or opportunity? How might this be part of a plan that you can't see right now? Take these doubts to God in prayer and let Him ease your mind.

13

RUN FOR THE PRIZE

Do you not know that in a race all the runners run, but only one gets the prize? Run in such a way as to get the prize. Everyone who competes in the games goes into strict training. They do it to get a crown that will not last, but we do it to get a crown that will last forever.

1 Corinthians 9:24–25

I'm not a runner. I'm built for strength, not for speed. Distance running has always been tough for me. Get me on a basketball court and I'll run for hours on end, because I absolutely love basketball. But running in a straight path makes me feel like I'm going to faint. Though I've run multiple marathons, 10Ks, and 5Ks in my life, I must train for them ahead of time. That training helps build my endurance so that I can persevere.

Training takes discipline and consistency. You must show up day in and day out regardless of how you feel or what's going on in your life. This builds mental toughness. Most importantly, it prepares you for the race that will come. Physical fitness helps us get stronger, feel better, and prepares us for things we might face. Do you know what the best form of physical training is? It's the one you'll do consistently.

It doesn't matter what you do, as long as you're doing something. There's no quick fix or specific thing you need to be doing as long as you're being intentional and staying active. I tend to go through different seasons of physical training. In warm seasons, I find myself drawn to outdoor activities like hikes, walks, playing street ball, and going to the beach. During colder seasons, I migrate indoors to lift weights or compete in open gym basketball games.

One thing that's helped me continuously train is setting goals on my calendar. I'm more likely to show up when I'm training for something. A vacation, a trip, an event, a competition, or a date. I found that when I have a vision or direction, I'm more likely to follow through.

Father God, help me to be more intentional when it comes to my health and wellness. Teach me to steward this body in a manner that is pleasing to

You. I'm grateful for the body You've given me. I recognize that it has flaws and imperfections, but I want to maximize its potential by taking care of it. In Jesus' name, amen.

Answer the following questions in your journal: What are you training for? What are your goals? What drives you? Make time to clarify your *why* and jot down a few action steps you can take today that will help with your drive toward your fitness goals.

14

CONTENTMENT IN ALL CIRCUMSTANCES

But godliness with contentment is great gain.

1 Timothy 6:6

Wanting a nicer car, bigger home, or a better job isn't a bad or evil thing. Having ambition, drive, being a goal setter or a vision caster are all great characteristics and can be rooted in godliness. It becomes an issue when this is your driving force and you lose track of your greater purpose.

Contentment is a state of mental and emotional satisfaction with your current circumstances, possessions, or situations. It means you have a sense of peace, fulfillment, and acceptance of what you have without a constant desire for more or different things.

Are you content with what God has already given you? If you never had another prayer answered or received another thing from God, would you be okay with that? That's a tough question that should be pondered periodically.

I lived a life of discontentment for years. Nothing was enough. I always needed the latest and newest. It was a constant chase and hustle, which was exhausting. I realized that I was missing out on enjoying what I already had because I was so consumed with getting more. It's a waste of life.

As a born-again follower of Jesus, you can still have goals and dreams, but it is important to regularly run them through the filter of Christ. Ask yourself if these things are for you or for Him. If you don't get these things or reach these goals, how will it affect your faith? Are you missing out on godly things now in the pursuit of good things for later? Would you be willing to walk away from it if God asks you to?

I highly encourage you to regularly and honestly audit your visions, dreams, and goals to ensure that what you're going after is what God called you to. We can get distracted by good things in exchange for God things when we operate from discontent.

Lord, settle my heart. Wash over me with an ever-present peace and calm that comes only from knowing You. I lay down my visions, dreams, and goals and ask that You would close any doors that aren't from You. Put me back on the path You've laid out. I tend to lose focus. Help me to stay fixed on You. In Jesus' name, amen.

Write in your journal the things God has done for you that you're grateful for. Make another list of the things He is currently doing in your life. Stop and thank Him for His involvement and guidance.

15

AN UNSHAKABLE FUTURE

*Therefore, since we are receiving a kingdom that
cannot be shaken, let us be thankful, and so worship
God acceptably with reverence and awe.*

Hebrews 12:28

Recently, I spoke at a conference in North Carolina. The event was amazing, but I had to leave right after I finished my speaking engagement to catch my flight back to Los Angeles. I made sure I was ready to go and left with plenty of time to get to the airport. The airport was only twenty minutes from the venue, so I left an hour and a half before takeoff.

About five miles away from the airport, there was a horrible accident that completely shut down the highway

I was on. I couldn't reverse, cut around, or get off at the next exit. I was stuck. I watched my estimated time of arrival grow later and later as I sat helplessly in the car. Almost an hour crept by, and I realized I wasn't going to make my flight. I was frustrated, but not defeated. I got to the airport about twenty minutes after my flight departed and headed to the service desk. The woman helping me was understanding and got me on the next flight out, which was about ninety minutes later. It was inconvenient, but I made it home.

As I sat in traffic waiting to get to the airport, I went through a range of emotions. I was mad at the traffic, then mad at myself for not leaving earlier, then sad for whoever had been in the accident, then grateful that I didn't leave a little earlier because I could have been involved in that crash. It was an emotional rollercoaster.

What I learned in this experience is that we can plan, schedule, and prepare all we want, but God's plan will always prevail. His purpose will override ours 100 percent of the time. It's a reminder that having an unshakable faith for our future means being secure and confident in what lies ahead. God isn't caught off guard or shaken. He has already anticipated the minor inconveniences and details that are frustrating to us. God isn't shaken when things don't go our way—we shouldn't be either.

Father God, You are my solid rock and firm foundation. Thank You for never being shaken or moved. Help me to remember that when things aren't going my way, they're going Your way, and that's the way I want to go. Teach me to run to You when life seems out of whack. Help me to put my faith in Your plan. In Jesus' name, amen.

When was the last time you were inconvenienced or your plans were hindered? In retrospect, can you see God's hand in the incident? Take a moment to thank Him for His involvement in your life and future.

16

A GODLY EXAMPLE

As a father has compassion on his children, so the
LORD has compassion on those who fear him.

Psalm 103:13

I'm reminded daily of the love God has for me when I look at my kids. I'm imperfect, I make mistakes, I fall short, yet I love my kids and want what's best for them. If I, a deeply flawed man, have the capacity to look at my kids with compassion and a desire to see them succeed, how much more does our heavenly Father look at us with a love that is truly indescribable?

It's easy to forget who we are as children of God. We are overwhelmed daily with messages of who we should be, what we should strive toward, and how we should live our lives. Remember that if it's not found in the Bible or doesn't come from the mouth of God, then it's counterfeit.

Don't let the world define you as a person. You must reject the subliminal messages about your identity.

Come back to the truth of who you are daily through times of prayer, devotion, and by looking at the relationships God has allowed you to be in. Feeling the trust that the kids in your life have in you and witnessing their faith and belief that you're there for them and wouldn't steer them wrong is powerful. It's a constant reminder of the parent-child relationship God desires to have with those who've put their faith in Jesus.

Today, as your mind begins to wander away from the truth of who you are, remind yourself how much love and compassion the Lord has toward you so that you can be a godly example to your family.

> *Lord God, help me to see myself through Your eyes and not the limiting eyes of the world. Remind me of Your love, mercy, and grace that You extend to me daily. Help my mind to stay grounded on Your truth and not be led astray by the lies of the enemy. In Jesus' name, amen.*

Carve out a moment for silent reflection regarding who you are as a child of God. Jot down a few of the counterfeit identities you tend to believe about yourself. Then right after, write out who you are in Christ and how He sees you.

17

PLEASING GOD THROUGH FAITH

And without faith it is impossible to please God, because anyone who comes to him must believe that he exists and that he rewards those who earnestly seek him.

Hebrews 11:6

It is easy to have faith when things are going well. When life is good, the bills are paid, the sun is out, and there is no storm in sight, it is easy to believe that God is good. On the other hand, when unexpected invoices come in, tragedy strikes, our health is compromised, or the storm is blowing, we ask where God is.

"'You of little faith'" (Matthew 8:26). It's one thing to read about the disciples freaking out in the boat that is about to be capsized while Jesus is taking a nap, but it is another thing when you feel as if your life is about to sink. Nowhere in the Bible are we promised a life immune from issues and obstacles. We aren't guaranteed a carefree life or one that is filled with comfort and ease.

Life is going to throw you curveballs, and trouble is going to hit when you're not looking and kick you when you're down. But no matter how bad your circumstances get, your faith in Him must remain strong. God's character isn't based on our circumstances. Our faith in Him who is unchangeable can be firm even when everything around us is changing.

We can live in a way that pleases God by staying strong in our faith even when life is filled with calamity. This means not just believing that He exists but believing that He's good even when life isn't. How we respond to adverse situations speaks loudly about our faith. Are you rooted in deep truth or shallow misconceptions? Is your faith built on crisis or intimate relationship?

Take inventory on what your faith in God says about your relationship with Him. Is He your sovereign Savior or just a glorified genie you run to when you need something?

Father God, help me to live a life that is pleasing to You, a life that is built on trust and faith.

Teach me to walk with You through both good and bad times. Give me the discernment to see that regardless of what I'm facing, You're still in control. May You receive glory by how I live my life in faith. In Jesus' name, amen.

Analyze whether or not your faith wavers when you face hard or uncomfortable circumstances. Think through strategies that you can have in place when trouble hits, such as making a list of your favorite Scripture verses to have on hand when life is difficult or identifying a friend who can remind you of how trustworthy God is.

18

THE MARATHON OF FAITH

Therefore, since we are surrounded by such a great cloud of witnesses, let us throw off everything that hinders and the sin that so easily entangles. And let us run with perseverance the race marked out for us.

Hebrews 12:1

What's keeping you from running your race well? This is a question to ask yourself often. What things in your life are keeping you from being the best version of who God's called you to be? We want to give God our best, but we sometimes allow unimportant things to get in the way.

Reflecting constantly and taking regular inventory will help you keep your life free of things that cause you to stumble. As we age, there are things that we used to get away with that we no longer can. We can't eat everything we want, we can't get by on insufficient sleep, and we can't work out without first warming up.

When we don't adjust how we're treating our body, we use old techniques that no longer serve us. We need to fuel our body with the right foods. We need to eat more whole and nutrient dense foods, and we must get enough sleep to be productive. After every training session, we must take the time to stretch our muscles so that we don't get tight and sore.

Letting go of old strategies when we enter new seasons can be hard, but it's necessary. Take time to audit how you've been treating your body and let go of the things that are no longer working. Restructure your routine to fit your current age, level of health, and nagging injuries. We all want to finish well, so make the necessary changes to help you do so.

Lord, may Your name be glorified by how I finish this race. I can't do this without You. Show me how to honor You with the resources You've entrusted to me. Help me to audit and discard any out-of-date strategies I've employed. Teach me

*the importance of adjusting my routine so that
I can run this race with perseverance. In Jesus'
name, amen.*

Make a list of the actions you can take to improve your physical health. Include a potential hindrance to those goals. What act of kindness can you give your body that reflects Christ's love?

19

GIVING CHEERFULLY

Each of you should give what you have decided in your heart to give, not reluctantly or under compulsion, for God loves a cheerful giver.

2 Corinthians 9:7

The Church has traditionally used emotional manipulation, pressure, and guilt to get people to give financially. This is disheartening because it creates distrust for the institution of religion and the things of God. Greedy men and women inspired by an unholy spirit have taken advantage of the generosity of saints around the world for thousands of years. This was never God's original design.

Giving and generosity are necessary for the existence of the Church. God has given His people the resources they need both to live and to ensure the survival of the body. These resources aren't to be squeezed out of the people, but they are to be given in a way that is effortless, filled with faith, and joyful. Giving back should come with a sense of gratefulness, not guilt.

People have attempted to take what God has brought together and use it for their own selfish gain. We must get back to the place where generosity is celebrated. Where it is a gift and honor to do so because it glorifies God, the One who ultimately provides for us. We have an opportunity to bless others with what we've been blessed with. We can't allow the actions of a few people with bad intentions stop us from doing what we were made to do.

You might be a little skeptical of big organizations because it seems like the dollars get lost. If that is the case, you can find other ways to financially give back. Paying it forward in stores or places you see a need, buying someone's groceries, buying dinner for a large group or a family in need, or donating and tithing to a trusted church. There are many ways to be generous, to give back, and to honor God with your finances. If you like to write a check and be less involved, make sure to pray over your decision and ask God for guidance. You want to be confident and cheerful knowing that your dollars are making an impact on His Kingdom.

Dear Lord, bring back the joy to generosity. Give me opportunities to cheerfully give and make a difference in people's lives. Help me to steward what You've given me, and align me with the people, churches, and organizations You want to be a blessing to. Use me as an instrument of Your glory to impact the lives of those around me. In Jesus' name, amen.

Name the people or organizations you feel called to bless financially and take a step to do that today. What are some other ways you can express generosity? Take a minute to thank God for His generosity toward you.

20

ETERNAL PERSPECTIVE

For our light and momentary troubles are achieving for us an eternal glory that far outweighs them all. So we fix our eyes not on what is seen, but on what is unseen, since what is seen is temporary, but what is unseen is eternal.

2 Corinthians 4:17–18

When you're going through a challenging time, you can feel as if it is the end of the world. Let's be honest, life can pack a punch. Loss, hurt, heartbreak, grief, financial issues, health complications, the list goes on. They don't stop coming. Sometimes it can feel as though the storm is never-ending. How do we get back up after being knocked down time after time?

It is helpful to look at life through the lens of eternity. This perspective doesn't make us immune to the trials of life, but it equips us to handle trials in a healthy way. Our faith isn't based on an easy life free from pain—our faith is in the promise of eternity. Remind yourself that bad things happen to good people every day. This is the world we live in because of sin. But this was never God's original design.

Life is filled with pain. There's pain associated with birth, pain felt during life, and then pain as we experience death. Birth and death are not the beginning and the end; they're transitions. We transition painfully from the womb to life as we know it. We live lives that are filled with hurt and pain. Then we transition into eternity through the painful process of death. It's inevitable.

People are so consumed with living a life of comfort that is free from any suffering and distress that when hard issues arise, they get discouraged and take on the role of a victim. They start complaining that life isn't fair, and they lose track of what's most important.

The big picture is eternity. Our eyes should be set on Him, not our hurt. These momentary inconveniences and sufferings are a part of life that we all experience as we transition from this life to the next. When you get discouraged, remember what Jesus went through on your behalf. When we look at the suffering of our Savior, our circumstances become a whole lot more bearable.

God, help me to look at life through the lens of eternity and not the lens of my limitations. Help me to see that everyone is fighting battles that I have no idea about. When I start to feel sorry for myself, bring to my memory the suffering of my Savior and remind me that my circumstances pale in comparison. I pray this in the power of Jesus' name, amen.

What do you set your eyes on during hard times? What challenging things are you experiencing right now? How can remembering what Jesus went through for you help change your perspective?

21

YOUR FIRST MINISTRY

He must manage his own family well and see that his children obey him, and he must do so in a manner worthy of full respect. (If anyone does not know how to manage his own family, how can he take care of God's church?)

1 Timothy 3:4–5

Even though we know how valuable time is, we still allow the pressures of society to take away this precious commodity from the ones God desires us to spend it on. Work, career aspirations, and even an honest desire to provide cause many people to neglect their loved ones and give their best to things that ultimately don't matter.

Our first and most important ministry is our family. The people God has placed in our life or in our intimate sphere of influence are to be our highest priority, yet we often neglect them. We can have the greatest impact on those closest to us, but we often sacrifice our precious moments with them for things that have no eternal significance.

In 1 Timothy, we're reminded that our ability to lead starts in our inner circle and grows from there. It would be a shame to have a successful ministry or business but have a broken home. What is the point of having immense success but having no one to share it with?

There is a tension between trying to provide well for your family and spending quality time with them. Our desire to give our loved ones all the things we think they need to succeed in life can become the priority. After failing miserably at this in my own life, God brought it to my attention that the most important thing I was missing in my childhood wasn't material things but quality time with people who genuinely loved me.

It's tempting to believe that the sacrifice we make for our family is in their best interest. But ultimately, we know that the thing they need most is us. After all is said and done, what they'll remember most and what will have the greatest impact on them isn't the presents you give them, it's the presence you give them.

Father God, help me to see the importance of being present with those close to me. Help me not just to be aware but to take action. Change my perspective and transform the way I share my love with the ones You've placed in my care. Teach me to love others like You do. In Jesus' name, amen.

How are you dealing with the tension between providing for those you love and being present with them? What is one thing you can do to give your loved ones more time? What is one thing you can eliminate to create more space for others?

22

WALKING BY FAITH, NOT SIGHT

For we live by faith, not by sight.

2 Corinthians 5:7

You've probably heard it said that seeing is believing. When it comes to faith, however, that couldn't be more wrong. We're called to believe without seeing. We are to trust without knowing or understanding how things will play out and to step out into the unknown without being able to see what's in front of our noses. It's hard, and it can be scary!

God knows how challenging this can be, and He is patient with us. He takes our hand and walks with us step by step. He gently leads and nudges us forward. It's the fact that He is with us that makes it possible to live by faith without knowing what lies ahead.

No matter what happens on earth, our eternity is sealed. Death has been defeated. The enemy has been conquered. Our body may die, but our spirit will live on because of Jesus. With that in mind, we can be encouraged, strengthened, and have all fear disappear. When we are reminded of the bigger picture, that our comfort isn't the goal and we aren't the center of everything, we can walk boldly by faith.

When the heaviness of a situation starts to weigh you down or the gravity of a problem begins to suck you in, come back to the truth—our anchor in Christ and the Word. Our firm footing comes from standing on Scripture. It might be dark, and you may not be able to see what lies ahead, but remember you have the SON-light with you. He will guide your steps and illuminate the way you should go. When you hear His voice calling you to jump out into the unknown, remember that He'll be there to catch you.

Father God, You call us to walk by faith and not by sight. But sometimes my faith fails me. Take me by the hand, Lord, and lead me in Your ways. Teach me to obey, even when I can't see the road ahead. Help me to trust You in ways that don't make sense but that honor and glorify Your name. In Jesus' name, amen.

Has God called you to do something in an unfamiliar realm? Are there things you're hesitating to obey because you can't see the full picture? Take a minute and visualize God in the darkness with you holding your hand. Step out in faith knowing that He is with you!

23

REST IN CHRIST

"Come to me, all you who are weary and burdened, and I will give you rest. Take my yoke upon you and learn from me, for I am gentle and humble in heart, and you will find rest for your souls. For my yoke is easy and my burden is light."

Matthew 11:28–30

Rest is something I've never taken seriously, but it eventually caught up to me. I'm notorious for pushing myself to my physical limits, going full speed without a break, and not taking time to recharge. My background is in the fitness industry where we throw around sayings like, "No pain, no gain" or, "Keep grinding" or, "Go hard or go home." These catchphrases make for awesome T-shirts, but they're not sustainable mindsets.

Never allowing yourself to rest or recharge is the perfect recipe for disaster. There is a time for resilience, perseverance, pressing through, and sacrifice, but we must pay attention to the warning signs our body sends when it's had enough. When we ignore these signals, we run the risk of burning out. Rest is important!

Our bodies need rest to recover, recharge, and repair. Rest isn't a suggestion, it's a necessity. Often, we choose not to rest because we lack trust. We think that if we take time off, the thing we're working on will fall apart. Whether it's a physical, financial, or material goal, we are afraid that if we stop pushing forward, everything will crumble.

We must trust that God will cover us in our moments of rest. Our results won't be lost when we take a break. In fact, we will come back stronger and more focused. If we take time off, we will be reenergized and able to pour more into our professional and personal pursuits. When we surrender control and begin to understand that God is with us even when we rest, we start to see the value in taking time off.

Heavenly Father, I give You all my worries. I've operated in my own strength for too long. Give me a rest that comes only from having an intimate relationship with You. Renew me, recharge

me, and revitalize my spirit. Into Your hands I
submit my life because You are in total control.
I pray all this in the power of Jesus' name, amen.

In what areas in your life do you need to relinquish control? How has a lack of trust affected your performance? What specific burdens do you need to let go of and allow God to restore you through rest? Journal your answers to these questions.

24

WISDOM FOR FINANCIAL DECISIONS

How much better to get wisdom than gold, to get insight rather than silver!

Proverbs 16:16

One of the things I love to pray for is wisdom. Too often we ask God to change our situation when it would be more prudent for us to ask Him to change us. Wisdom, knowledge, understanding, and discernment are my top four asks when it comes to prayer. "Lord, give me the wisdom to respond." "Father, give me the wisdom to handle this in a manner that glorifies You." "God, I need wisdom to help me navigate this situation."

Many times, the answer to our prayers is right in front of us. We fail to see it because we're waiting for God to remove the situation rather than help us in it. When it comes to finances, we can ask God for wisdom to help us steward what we already have. We often expect God to multiply what we have when we haven't handled our existing resources wisely.

If we can't manage one thousand dollars, what makes us think we'll miraculously be able to manage one hundred thousand dollars? Getting more doesn't mean we become better stewards. Our character flaws and errors in stewardship will only be magnified. In every aspect of our lives, but especially finances, we should be asking God for the wisdom to steward well what He's entrusted to us.

When you ask for wisdom, you begin to see what you already have differently. You can make changes in how you spend, save, and invest. In all areas of your life, your aim should be to honor and glorify God. Handling your finances in an unwise or careless way is a poor reflection of your relationship with God. Whether or not you've been careless with your finances, ask God for the wisdom to spend, save, and invest in ways that honor Him.

> *Lord,* I pray for wisdom, knowledge, under-
> standing, and discernment. Open my eyes to the
> error of my ways and reveal to me any area where
> I'm not being a good steward. Help me to make

the changes necessary to live a life that brings honor to You. Have Your way in my finances and teach me to multiply what You've entrusted to my care. In Jesus' name, amen.

To what degree do you feel you have submitted your finances to God? In what ways are you still holding on to control? Write down a few ways that you can practically begin to honor Him in your finances. Ask Him to show you ways to spend, save, and invest that give Him glory.

25

ASSURANCE OF GOD

And we know that in all things God works for the good of those who love him, who have been called according to his purpose.

Romans 8:28

At the end of the day, God knows best. Trials, tribulations, obstacles, issues, hurt, pain, valleys, and grief all make sense in Him. We have such a hard time understanding the point of life, and many times we stray away from the ultimate meaning. When times get tough, we like to question God as if He forgot about us or left us behind. That's not His nature. That's not who He is. Our circumstances don't dictate who He is. Just because we're having a bad day doesn't mean that God is bad. If we're having a good day, that doesn't increase His goodness. God is the same yesterday, today, and forever (see Hebrews 13:8).

All things work together for the good of those who love Him (see Romans 8:28). Not some things, not a few things, not just the good things, *all* things. God is good! He is perfect and righteous and holy, and even in the middle of the storm, He loves you. Our confidence should not be based on an absence of problems, but based on knowing that our God is with us through them all.

We go through difficult situations, and in those times, we struggle with understanding that all things work out for our good. That's why we must stand firm on the Word of God and not allow our feelings to be louder than our faith. Run to the Word in moments that seem too hard and remind yourself that God says all things are for your good. If God says *all* things, then we must trust that even when we don't see it, He's working. He's fighting battles on our behalf that we have no idea about. You can rest in God's promises.

Father God, sometimes I allow my feelings to be louder than my faith. I let the issues strangle out the truth and get overwhelmed. Remind me of Your love, Your mercy, and Your grace. Teach me to see things from Your point of view. Help me remember there's no mountain too big that can stand in the way of Your love. In Jesus' name, amen.

What situations in your life right now are currently overwhelming? Along with Romans 8:28, run to the Word and find two more verses that give you peace. Meditate on those verses today.

26

HANDING DOWN LESSONS

My son, keep your father's command and do not forsake your mother's teaching. Bind them always on your heart; fasten them around your neck. When you walk, they will guide you; when you sleep, they will watch over you; when you awake, they will speak to you.

Proverbs 6:20–22

Not having a father figure growing up taught me lessons that were invaluable. It shaped the way I parent my own kids. I've thought about what it would have been like to grow up with a dad, but I understand things happened the way God intended. Rather than learning how to be a good man, I learned how not to be. Although these lessons were hard to learn and came with many challenges, I'm grateful to be able to pass down a new legacy. I can be the father I never had.

In the same way, we can hand down lessons and pass on knowledge to the next generation. The question is, what are you teaching them? Most lessons in life aren't taught with words—they're caught with actions. Kids have the irritating attribute of modeling and following what they see. We can talk until we're blue in the face and try to teach through words, but if our actions don't line up with what we're preaching, it usually goes in one ear and out the other.

You might be able to relate to this. How many times did leaders, coaches, or other adults try to instill wisdom into you, but they weren't modeling it themselves? If you ever experienced this, it's a great reminder that we need to be careful and intentional. We can't expect those we're trying to lead to do things we aren't willing to do. If you want to have an impact on the ones you love, make sure you're leading with your life so the lessons you're handing down will live on.

> *Heavenly Father,* *teach me to be not just a hearer of the Word, but a doer of the Word. Help me to lead from experience. Just as Jesus came to show us the way, help me to hand down life*

*lessons by being the change I desire to see. In
Jesus' name, amen.*

How well do you feel your words line up with your
actions? Think about ways those two things diverge in
your life. Write down a few thoughts about how you can
be consistent with your words and actions.

27

FULLY PERSUADED IN FAITH

Yet he did not waver through unbelief regarding the promise of God, but was strengthened in his faith and gave glory to God, being fully persuaded that God had power to do what he had promised.

Romans 4:20–21

God is working even when we don't see it. He is fighting battles on our behalf that we know nothing about. He is opening doors that only He can open and shutting down opportunities that would lead us astray. We can't begin to know the depths and inner workings of our Lord. His ways are above ours.

When things don't look the way you expected them to look, remind yourself that God knows best. If something isn't going your way, it's going His way, and that's always the best way. Hold on to His promises when you don't understand what's happening.

What are the promises you hold on to? What verses have you written on your heart that you run to in times of need? For me it's the promise that God will never leave me nor forsake me. As a child, I often felt abandoned or discarded, so I wrestle with reoccurring thoughts that God has walked away from me. This promise strengthens my faith and serves as a constant reminder.

Just because we can't see how He's working doesn't mean that He isn't. Let His promises and character be the foundation on which you walk in faith. He'll never fail you. He is faithful, merciful, kind, consistent, on time, and doesn't lie. You won't waver in your faith when you stand on the truth of who God is.

Heavenly Father, help me to see You for who You are. Help me to see Your truths in this world that is filled with lies. Teach me to hold on to Your promises when the world offers me counterfeit substitutions that only You can provide. Strengthen my faith in You so that I'm not so easily knocked off track with every inconvenience. In Jesus' name, amen.

What promises from God are you holding on to? In times of confusion, what are you holding on to for stability? Take time to reflect on those promises that are anchors for your soul. Write out at least two of them, post them in prominent places, and read them in the morning and evening.

28

RENEW YOUR MIND

Do not conform to the pattern of this world, but be transformed by the renewing of your mind. Then you will be able to test and approve what God's will is—his good, pleasing and perfect will.

Romans 12:2

The world we live in is self-centered, self-seeking, filled with comparison, and out of alignment with how God designed us to live. It's easy to be distracted and sidetracked by things that are unimportant. It takes work to constantly bring our mind back to God's plan for our lives.

We weren't created to fit in, to keep up with our neighbors, or to live for the next big experience. That's the lie that many of us fall for. We're consumed by trends of what is popular and what's new. We weren't saved to sit on the sidelines and merely survive. Renewing our mind takes intentionality and a willingness to fight against the current of the world. God wants to use us, our life experiences, and our unique qualities to make His name known and glorified in all the earth. It can be challenging to do that when we're consumed with ourselves and our comfort.

It is only when we're brutally honest with ourselves, when we weigh our intentions and check our heart posture regularly, that we are able to remain focused.

Remember that renewing your mind is an ongoing journey, and it may take time. Be patient with yourself and consistent in your efforts. Small changes in your thought patterns can lead to significant improvements in your mental well-being over time.

> *Dear God, help me stay focused on You. Renew my mind daily and help me remember the plan, purpose, and will You have for my life. I want to glorify You with how I spend my time, energy, effort, and resources. Teach me to turn down the noise of this world and to tune in to Your voice. In Jesus' name, amen.*

Which do you find yourself more concerned about: the things of the world or the things of the Lord? How much do you wrestle with comparison or feeling as if you're missing out on things because of your service to Him? Jot down the things of the world that attract you. Write down what you feel you're missing out on. Then give those things to the Lord.

29

AVOIDING THE LOVE OF MONEY

For the love of money is a root of all kinds of evil. Some people, eager for money, have wandered from the faith and pierced themselves with many griefs.

1 Timothy 6:10

Talking about money can sometimes get a little awkward, especially in church. People have so many wrong ideas when it comes to money and God. This Scripture verse has been misquoted hundreds of times, most often as "Money is the root of all evil!" But it's the love of money that's the root of evil, not money itself. We've all seen headlines of high-profile preachers being accused of money laundering, tax evasion, or fraud. They're walled up in their ten-bedroom mansions and flying around in their private jets while their congregations are struggling to survive. Money and the church don't seem to go well together.

This shouldn't be the case. Money is a very real part of life and a necessity. We need it to live, to eat, to secure shelter, to use transportation, and to function every day. There's no way around it, so we have to talk about it. As the Bible says, it is the love of money that is the root of evil. This makes sense, because God wants our love to be for Him, not money.

So, if money is necessary but the love of it is evil, how do we avoid falling in love with it? The answer is simple. We give it away. Generosity is one of the greatest measuring sticks to see where your loyalties lie. Tithing, donating, contributing, or giving it away, letting it go demonstrates the hold money does or does not have on your life. There's no greater antidote to greed than the regular practice of disciplined generosity.

As a young person, I had a hard time trusting the Church because I didn't grow up attending. Generosity was foreign to me, and the concept of giving when I barely had anything felt scary. What I found was that when I gave to God and His people, my heart felt right. I was able to be a blessing to someone else and to God's Kingdom. This feeling was contagious, and I found myself searching for ways to continue to give back. It's important to be a generous giver by cutting ties with your allegiance to money. This helps to guard your heart from the love of money.

> *Father God, my allegiance is to You. Break the ties and stronghold money has had on my life. Teach me to be a cheerful and generous giver. Show how Your heart rejoices when we reach into what You've given us to help others experience Your love. May Your name be glorified with how I steward my finances. In Jesus' name, amen.*

What is your belief around the use and accumulation of money? (Are you a keeper of money? Do you love money? Do you feel you need money to be happy? Are you a generous giver?) What is one way you can avoid falling in love with money? Answer these questions, and then ask God to reset any skewed thoughts you may unknowingly have.

30

HOPE FOR TOMORROW

May the God of hope fill you with all joy and peace as you trust in him, so that you may overflow with hope by the power of the Holy Spirit.

Romans 15:13

In my lifetime, I've put my hope in a lot of things instead of God. I have put my hope in people who have let me down. I have put my hope in opportunities that have fallen apart. I have put my hope in money but still felt empty. The things the world offers are counterfeit. Nothing came close to the genuine hope I found in God. Now I feel a profound sense of trust, assurance, and optimism that stems from my faith, which gives me comfort, peace, and purpose.

The only One in life who will show up time after time and never let you down is God. In Him, there is peace and joy that makes no sense to the world. Our hope is in the fact that our sins are forgiven, that we have access to our heavenly Father, and that we are saved. We can have a joy that comes from something that can't be taken away from us.

Happiness and joy are different. Happiness is influenced by circumstances, achievements, and daily experiences. Joy, on the other hand, is a more profound and intense emotion. It comes from experiencing Jesus, and it isn't something that goes away because we are having a bad day. It's a part of our identity as born-again followers of Jesus.

Peace and joy are available to us in Christ. We must operate in that knowledge. Every day, we will be faced with the decision to either surrender to our flesh and be overwhelmed by what we're going through, or to live in the Spirit and choose peace and joy during the hard times. What are you choosing? Are you operating out of emotion or your identity?

Lord, help me to see the peace and joy that are available in You. Teach me not to be so easily moved by my emotions and feelings. Ground me in Your Word and establish me on Your firm foundation. Show me how to keep my eyes fixed on Your unchanging love, mercy, and grace. In Jesus' name, amen.

Think about the situations that overwhelm you. How can knowing that peace and joy are available to you help calm you? Read Romans 15:13 a few times. Also, look up two more verses that speak to the peace and joy that we have access to in Him and journal about them.

31

DON'T BE SO HARD

Children, obey your parents in everything, for this pleases the Lord. Fathers, do not embitter your children, or they will become discouraged.

Colossians 3:20–21

Why do we take out our frustrations on the ones who are closest to us? Maybe you can relate. You've had a long day at work and come home exhausted, just wanting to get some food and relax. You get in the house, and your spouse, who has had an equally exhausting day, barely acknowledges your presence. The kids are wound up, bouncing off the walls and at each other's throats.

It's as if your home is a war zone and you just stepped on a land mine. There's tension rising, and the noise is migraine-inducing. As the conflict reaches the point of tears, you snap and lash out at the whole house because you just want a little peace and quiet. The atmosphere shifts. You got the quiet you desired, but at what cost? The kids are sad, scared, and discouraged. Your spouse is frustrated and disappointed and now has to do damage control.

This is an all-too-familiar situation that takes place in homes around the world. You may not resonate with the antagonist of the story, but maybe you saw yourself in the spouse, or even one of the kids. No matter where you see yourself in the illustration, the point is how easy it can be to take out all of your frustration on the ones who love you most.

How do we avoid situations like this? Through healthy communication. Tell your family what you need. Ask them what they need. Having a family huddle when you get home allows you to communicate intentions and expectations and come up with a plan of action. Give everyone a role and make them feel as if they're a part of a team.

In many instances families spell love T-I-M-E. Be intentional about taking time to touch base with each person and really focus on not being so hard on them. Unless we ask, we don't know what kind of day they have had.

Father God, help me to operate in the love, patience, and grace I have in Christ Jesus. Teach me to be gentle and not to provoke my family to anger with my actions. I want to be a source of comfort for my loved ones and not a source of bitterness. Fill my heart with Your love. In Jesus' name, amen.

Map out a rhythm for your home that takes into consideration each member's schedule and needs. Discuss that plan with your family. Make another plan for yourself for when your environment isn't ideal so that you can avoid lashing out at those you love.

32

STEPPING INTO THE UNKNOWN

By faith Abraham, when called to go to a place he would later receive as his inheritance, obeyed and went, even though he did not know where he was going.

Hebrews 11:8

I've always wrestled with social anxiety. Going to new places by myself stirs up a nervousness that's reminiscent of the first day of school. My palms get clammy, I get short of breath, and I sit back and observe before I get comfortable enough to interact. If I'm with someone I know, however, it's a whole different story. Being with a friend or family member gives me a confidence that I wouldn't usually have on my own. I have someone to talk to. I can play off his or her energy and confidence. It takes the focus off of me, which gives me space to breathe.

In the same way, when I journey into the unknown by myself, without the guidance of God, it can be terrifying. My head is filled with questions, concerns, and confusion. Should I be here? Is this God's plan? Am I on my own? On the other hand, when I hear clear instruction from God, the unknown is less intimidating. I have confidence and authority because the Lord is with me, has gone before me, and is fighting by my side.

A few things I do that help me solidify whether or not something is from God so that I can confidently move forward include confirming it with Scripture, seeking godly advice or counseling, and asking God for clarity. Through prayer, advice, and Scripture you can get the answers you're looking for so you can walk boldly into the unknown with the confidence that God is by your side.

Lord, as I march forward in obedience and trust, I know that You are with me. I ask that You'd close any doors that You wouldn't have me walk through. Illuminate my path and give me the boldness that comes from knowing You are by my side. In Jesus' name, amen.

Imagine yourself going into a difficult or complicated situation alone. Then imagine that same situation with God encouraging you and Jesus walking alongside you. Journal about your thoughts and feelings in both situations.

33

EMPOWERED FOR ENDURANCE

I can do all this through him who gives me strength.

Philippians 4:13

The only way we finish this race well is with the strength and power of the Lord. On our own, we can accomplish some pretty good things. But if we want to accomplish God things, we need God's strength. I've racked up awards, achievements, and accolades that I'm proud of, but none of them compares to the lives that have been changed by His power through the works He has entrusted me to do.

We all have the desire to leave a mark on this world. We want to be remembered for the people we have touched and had a positive impact on. There is nothing more powerful than introducing someone to our life-changing Savior, Jesus Christ, and that can only be done in Him.

Life is filled with things that seem impossible. And in most instances without Him, they are. That's the beauty of a life surrendered to His Lordship; we can do things that don't make sense. He can open doors we never thought possible, He can make a path in the wilderness that surpasses our understanding, and He can provide in ways that blow our mind.

If God called you to it, He'll bring you through it, even if you can't wrap your head around how. Let this serve as a reminder that His ways are greater than ours. Let your faith be louder than your fear. When you find yourself with your back against the wall and you're unsure of how you can possibly endure, remember that in Him you can do all things.

In what ways have you allowed your limitations to be projected onto God? Don't forget that He has no limitations.

Father God, my strength can only take me so far. I'm reminded of my weakness daily because what You ask of me is impossible on my own. Teach me to be reliant upon You and Your abilities. Help me to stop disqualifying myself based

*on my limitations and to keep my mind fixed on
You. You are a way maker, and I put my trust in
You and Your power. In Jesus' name, amen.*

When has God's strength been sufficient in your life?
How easy is it for your fear to become louder than your
faith? What steps can you take to be more reliant on Him
and stop yourself from getting in the way of what He's
trying to do? Write those steps in your journal.

34

THE BLESSING OF GIVING

A generous person will prosper; whoever refreshes others will be refreshed.

Proverbs 11:25

One of the great parts about being a follower of Jesus is the ability and opportunity to have an impact on the lives of others. Helping others when they are in a time of need fosters human connection, shows empathy, and strengthens bonds. It's so rewarding when God uses us as a conduit for Him to bless His people. It strengthens our faith, and it helps us feel more connected, seen, and heard. Giving both time and money reflects a generous and compassionate spirit, and it allows us to extend kindness and support to others in need.

I'm thankful for the way I grew up because I got to experience firsthand what it's like to receive people's generosity. People bought our groceries, gave us money, and gifted us with things we needed. I understand the impact that giving can make. This has taught me to be the hands and feet of Jesus by being a blessing to others who are currently experiencing similar circumstances. I believe that God allows us to go through certain things that will help us better empathize with others so that we can eventually be a source of refreshment to them.

There's more happiness and joy to be found in God when we give rather than when we receive. Giving makes us more Christlike, which not only draws us closer to God, but also strengthens our faith and instills gratitude. Find ways to sow seeds and be a blessing to those who need to feel God's love.

> *Heavenly Father, I know that Your good and perfect will always will prevail. Help me to see Your hand in the grand design of my life and guide me in the way in which You're calling me. May Your name be glorified by the way I love others. Teach me to use my experiences and pain as*

points of empathy and connection with those less fortunate. In Jesus' name, amen.

Ask God to give you creative ideas of how to be a blessing to someone else. These are seeds that you can sow. Write down what you hear Him saying, and act on one of those ideas today.

35

IT'S IN GOD'S HANDS

*In their hearts humans plan their course, but the
LORD establishes their steps.*

Proverbs 16:9

This verse brings me peace and comfort. We have had
things fail and fall apart, but knowing circumstances
went God's way and not our own way can give us comfort. This can be hard to accept, though. When you put
in the effort and set a goal, you want everything to go
according to your plan. When that doesn't happen, you
may feel as if you've failed.

The beauty of serving God is that even His answer of
no has goodness written all over it. We can rest knowing
that if things don't work out the way we wanted them to,
it's for a good reason. We know that closed doors and
failed plans are ultimately for our protection or redirec-

tion. Our failed plans also keep us from settling for less than God has for us.

Standing on this truth can give us the courage and boldness to step out in faith and take calculated risks. Since God will establish our steps, we have the freedom to try things that might be intimidating or seem impossible. If our plan works out, our faith is increased, and we are strengthened. If the plans don't work, then it wasn't a part of His plan for us, and we have to accept that and keep moving forward.

We can't allow unfulfilled dreams, plans that fell apart, or visions that didn't come to pass to discourage us. When we know who He is and how much He loves us, we should be reminded to confidently make plans, set goals, and write down our vision. Remember that if we're led in a different direction, we are still walking in God's plan. If our plans are not from Him, we don't want them. That reminder can change our perspective on things not going our way. It's either His way or the highway.

Dear God, I've made plans and set goals that never came to pass. I know that it was because You love me and want what's best for me. If something I'm pursuing isn't from You, I don't want it. Teach me to stay close to the path You've laid out in front of me. Help me to follow You closely. In Jesus' name, amen.

Write in your journal the plans you are currently pursuing. Ask God to confirm those plans He has initiated and show you if any of those plans are not in His will. Let go of the plans that are not for you and focus on those that are.

36

RAISING UP WARRIORS

Children are a heritage from the Lord, offspring a reward from him. Like arrows in the hands of a warrior are children born in one's youth. Blessed is the man whose quiver is full of them. They will not be put to shame when they contend with their opponents in court.

Psalm 127:3–5

Having kids is a blessing. Whether you're a biological parent, an adoptive parent, a stepparent, a godparent, or the really cool aunt or uncle, your role in the lives of little ones is important. They are our future leaders! So being intentional in how we raise them is critical.

To be likened to arrows in the hand of a warrior is a powerful illustration. An arrow is propelled forward by the power and aim of the one who is handling the bow.

It's our privilege to empower, inspire, and send forward the little ones in our sphere of influence. How are we bringing them in, building them up, and sending them out?

Today, the cultural norm is to raise your kid to the age of eighteen so that you can get them out of the house and enjoy yourself. We're missing out on the opportunity to instill good values, character, and integrity in the next generation. When we sit and complain about all the chaos in the world and how we don't have good leadership to help us navigate through the calamity, we can't blame anyone but ourselves. The leaders of today are the product of our failures.

Don't miss out on the precious moments and opportunities to sharpen the arrows you've been entrusted with. Remember that raising warriors is about nurturing well-rounded individuals who have developed the skills and qualities needed to face life's challenges with courage and resilience. Lead by example, live a life you'd want to see duplicated, and spend time with the children in your life. Be genuine, vulnerable, and transparent. Children are a reward, not a burden. Make it a point to speak life, strength, and direction into them every chance you get.

Lord, I thank You for the opportunities I have to shape, mold, and inspire the future generations.

Help me to sharpen them, build them up, and send them forward in Your name. Teach me to lead a life I'd want to see duplicated, which is a life of obedience to You. May Your name be honored. In Jesus' name, amen.

Think through the key children who are in your life (your own plus those closest to you) and write their names down. Take a moment to pray for each of them by name, and then write out some strategies of how you can intentionally invest in their lives. If there is a specific action you feel called to take, make plans to take that action today.

37

WALKING IN FAITHFUL OBEDIENCE

But Samuel replied: "Does the LORD delight in burnt offerings and sacrifices as much as in obeying the LORD? To obey is better than sacrifice, and to heed is better than the fat of rams."

1 Samuel 15:22

You can dedicate your entire life to doing "good works" for God, but if you don't obey when He's asking you to do something, you're still being disobedient. The "good works" mindset and heart posture ruins religion. It's a works-based posture where if you do the "right" religious things then God is pleased.

While we all make different sacrifices for God, He values obedience and adherence to His commands more than external acts of worship, rituals, or sacrifices. This verse emphasizes the importance of following God's instructions completely and sincerely rather than attempting to make up for disobedience through offerings. Making sacrifices in your life may include giving up certain things for God for the sake of a greater good or higher purpose.

I had to learn this the hard way. I thought if I went to church, said the right things, helped at outreach events, and made the right sacrifices, I was walking faithfully in obedience. I thought I was building my relationship with God this way. I couldn't have been more wrong! I knew the Bible, but I didn't know Jesus. I had no idea who He truly was or what He wanted me to do. My actions and thoughts were far from Him, and I had no idea what obeying Him meant. I wasn't aware that being obedient to the Word of God is essential for maintaining a close and intimate relationship with Him because it involves actively seeking and following divine guidance in all aspects of my life.

Obedience takes faith. To follow God and be guided by Him when you don't know where you'll end up requires obedience. You can't have one without the other. Faith demonstrates your trust in the wisdom and goodness of God's commandments, even when your understanding may be limited. A life that is pleasing to God is rooted in obedience, so don't get caught up in playing a part.

Lord, search my heart and help me to identify the areas where I've allowed religious sacrifice to be more important than obeying Your voice. Help me to hear You better. Teach me to pay attention to Your leadership. Forgive me for my disobedience and show me how to live a life that pleases You. In Jesus' name, amen.

Make a list of the things you're currently doing for God. Think about each one to analyze if they're good works or works done out of obedience. What have you been asked to do that you're hesitating on? Where does the hesitation come from? Write in your journal regarding these thoughts.

38

RESTORATION AND REVIVAL

He refreshes my soul. He guides me along the right paths for his name's sake.

Psalm 23:3

Many of us are running through life on empty. We're barely scraping by and doing everything we can to survive. This is normal behavior in our culture, and to do otherwise is often considered lazy and careless. Yet we weren't created to stumble through life like mindless, programmed zombies.

When's the last time you took a vacation? And I mean a real vacation, not a trip that is overbooked with attractions, to-do lists, and itineraries. Many people take a vacation and need a break when they get back home from what was supposed to be a restful trip. They come back sunburnt, dehydrated, sore, and more exhausted than when they left. It can be hard to shake that go-go-go mentality.

We weren't created to operate on go mode 24/7. We need rest. We need real pauses in our days. There's nothing bad, lazy, or careless about that. In fact, not getting enough rest is truly reckless. Somehow, we've learned to celebrate the ones who drag themselves across the finish line without an ounce of strength left in their body.

This is your official permission slip to take time to unplug and get the rest you need. You can't pour out of an empty cup. We must be intentional about taking time away from the hustle and bustle of daily living and get connected to our true source of strength. Even if you can't get away for an extended period, start scheduling time throughout the week to connect with the One who gives you strength.

What I've started to do is block off a day on my weekly calendar to ensure I don't schedule anything that day. I've communicated to my wife, family, and loved ones that this is something I need regularly to be the best version of myself. It seemed selfish at first, but once they saw how refreshed and well-rested I became, they got on board and are supportive when I take time away for myself.

Lord, I'm guilty of burning the candle at both ends. I often neglect time away with You and moments of being refreshed. Help me to be more intentional about unplugging from the world and plugging into You. You are my true source of rejuvenation. Teach me to trust You in every aspect of my life. In Jesus' name, amen.

What are your reactions to this message of rest? Are there hidden influencers that tell you that rest is selfish? Journal those thoughts. Does your present schedule allow for rest? If not, what can you move or cancel to ensure that you have time to refresh your soul?

39

THE SOURCE OF WEALTH

But remember the L<small>ORD</small> your God, for it is he who gives you the ability to produce wealth.

Deuteronomy 8:18

Everything comes from God; nothing is ours alone. We are merely stewards of what He has entrusted to us. We sometimes forget that we have only what He has allowed. We can get caught up in pride thinking that we've done something to deserve the things we have, but it's all because of God's never-ending love. It's easy to fall into the trap of entitlement, thinking everything we have is because we worked hard for it instead of recognizing that God gave it to us. When we lose sight of Jesus as our provider, we start to believe that the good things we have in our life are solely because of our actions or behavior. That undermines the truth of who our heavenly Father is. He is the master of your life, not you.

Even if God never gave us another thing, we already have everything—His Son, Jesus. That is the greatest gift of all. The blood sacrifice of Jesus who died on the cross paved the way for our sins to be forgiven. By putting our faith in Jesus Christ, we don't have to experience eternal separation from God. Nothing compares to that. We are blessed beyond measure.

Let's not forget that our creative minds that help us succeed were given to us by God. Our strong bodies that power us through grueling labor to provide for our families were given to us by God. That million-dollar idea was planted in your mind by God. That artistic talent and gift you use to make ends meet was placed in you by God. Nothing we have comes from us.

God deserves all the praise and glory in every aspect of our lives. We sometimes forget to thank Him and give credit where credit is due. This world is filled with self-promotion and pride. Let's get back to being humble and realizing that God is our source and the only One worthy of exultation. It all comes from Him.

Father God, help me to stay humble. Remind me that You formed me in my mother's womb. You put every aspect of who I am together with Your plan and purpose in mind. Teach me to honor and glorify You every chance I get. I wasn't designed to be worshiped, so help me point people to You when praiseworthy moments present themselves. In Jesus' name, amen.

How easy is it to slip into pride over your accomplishments and forget that Jesus is your provider? Look up a couple of verses that help you remember that everything comes from Him, write them down, and display them in a prominent place. Journal your thoughts about what those verses mean to you and refer to them often.

40

INCHING TOWARD THE FINISH LINE

I press on toward the goal to win the prize for which God has called me heavenward in Christ Jesus.

Philippians 3:14

I'm sure you have heard the story of the Tortoise and the Hare, the race where the slow-moving and consistent tortoise is pitted against the speedy hare. At the beginning of the race, the hare is running circles around the tortoise, expending all his energy, trying to be funny and show his confidence in winning the race. But after acting this way throughout the race, he tires himself out near the end. The tortoise ends up passing him and winning the race. The moral of the story is that it's not how you start, it is how you finish.

We can learn a lot of lessons from this story but none more important than the fact that life is a marathon. We must set a pace, stick to it, and finish well. I'm thankful that the finish is more important than the beginning. I didn't get a great start in life. I wasn't handed a silver spoon, I didn't inherit a trust fund, I wasn't born to middle-class working parents who loved me. I was born into addiction, poverty, and extreme dysfunction. The trajectory of my life was headed in the wrong direction before I was born.

Jesus rescued and then redirected us. He put us on the right path and now sets the pace at which we run. This world is fast-paced, and it is so easy to get caught up in its current. We have to be intentional about taking time to slow down, reflecting on the direction we're going, and being sure we're living at a pace that is sustainable.

We want to finish well. That means we must make sure we're not running in our own strength and endurance. We need to know we're on the path that God called us to. We must not expend our energy on things that aren't a part of His purpose.

Dear Lord, I want to finish well. Show me how to walk with You and to live in perfect union with Your Spirit. Teach me how to recognize when I'm out of step and off the path You've called me to.

Help me to run this race at a sustainable pace, and lead me to the finish line for Your glory. In Jesus' name, amen.

Take some time today to examine the way you're running. To what degree are you in step with the Lord? Are you sprinting when you should be jogging? How are you using your time, energy, and resources on what God has or hasn't assigned to you? Journal your thoughts.

41

THE FAMILY GOD GIVES

Then Jesus' mother and brothers arrived. Standing outside, they sent someone in to call him. A crowd was sitting around him, and they told him, "Your mother and brothers are outside looking for you." "Who are my mother and my brothers?" he asked. Then he looked at those seated in a circle around him and said, "Here are my mother and my brothers! Whoever does God's will is my brother and sister and mother."

Mark 3:31–35

My home life growing up could be characterized as dysfunctional. You may be able to relate. No home is perfect, and all have an element of chaos, it just varies by degree. One of the most beautiful parts of being adopted into the body of Christ is the family that comes with it. Family doesn't always mean blood relatives. In many instances, the people we choose to spend our lives with become our family.

God knows the brokenness that we have to endure in this fallen world, so He places people in our lives to help heal those wounds. We've been given spiritual fathers, mothers, brothers, and sisters who have helped us grow in ways we never thought possible.

A body has so many different moving parts and pieces. Similarly, being part of a family can also have its challenges. It requires you to get out of your comfort zone. You must let people have access to your heart. For some of us, that can be difficult. It requires trust. Not everyone has good intentions. Being part of a family, whether your family of origin or your chosen family, can become messy and isn't without issues, but it's worth it.

The goal isn't to replace the family you were born into, it's to recognize that God will intentionally place people in your life who can be vital parts in your growth and development as a believer.

Lord, thank You for the family of believers I'm surrounded with. Help me to nourish and cultivate deep and meaningful relationships that bring honor and glory to Your name. Teach me to see how You supply all my needs and equip me through Your Spirit, Your Word, and through others. May Your name receive the praise and the glory. In Jesus' name, amen.

Take inventory of the people in your life outside of your blood-born family. Do you have spiritual family? These are people who you've allowed to access parts of your life that are reserved for only the closest. How have they made you better? How have they encouraged you? If you don't have people like that in your life, pray that God would bring individuals into your life with whom you can create a family.

42

FAITHFUL IN THE SMALL THINGS

"Whoever can be trusted with very little can also be trusted with much, and whoever is dishonest with very little will also be dishonest with much."

Luke 16:10

When we ask God for more than what we already have, He evaluates how we've handled what He's already given us. How have we stewarded the gifts and responsibilities He has entrusted to us? Many times, we get caught up in our culture where consumerism, material belongings, and the desire for more guide our decisions. It's the world we live in! It's everywhere.

We're called, however, to be in the world but not of the world, so our perspective should be different. If we can't responsibly handle one thousand dollars, why do we think we'd do better with ten thousand? If we don't take care of the ten-year-old car we have, why do we think we'll take better care of a brand-new vehicle? We tend to believe that when we have something of greater value, we'll steward it better. While that may be true for a season, old habits and mindsets will eventually catch up with us.

We must take care of the things we have in a way that honors the Lord. Steward and handle well the influence you have now so that God can entrust you with more. Use the finances you have with wisdom so that when your dollar amount grows, the wisdom you've earned will allow you to continue to handle it well. Consistent faithfulness in small tasks and responsibilities builds trust and develops and strengthens our character.

With great power comes great responsibility. The character trait of being responsible has to come before increased power. The person who gains much power without having character is in for some serious learning opportunities—or failures. So let us learn now.

Father God, help me to steward well the things You've placed in my control. Teach me to use my time, energy, effort, and resources to glorify Your name. Expand my territory, reach, and sphere of influence. Show me how to be a trustworthy servant who operates out of wisdom and under-standing. In Jesus' name, amen.

What have you been entrusted with that requires you to steward it well and with wisdom? How well are you handling your current responsibilities? Do you think you could be trusted with more? If not, be intentional about how you're using your God-given gifts, talents, and resources.

43

DISCIPLINE AND DEDICATION

Whatever you do, work at it with all your heart, as working for the Lord, not for human masters, since you know that you will receive an inheritance from the Lord as a reward. It is the Lord Christ you are serving.

Colossians 3:23–24

Every task we do should be performed as if we're doing it for Jesus Himself, because we are. Everything we do can be done to honor Him. We shouldn't view the things we're required to do as an obligation but as an opportunity to glorify the Lord. Going to work is an opportunity to glorify the Lord. Taking care of your family is an opportunity to glorify the Lord. Taking care of your health is an opportunity to glorify the Lord.

Taking care of ourselves sometimes feels as if it is an obligation because it can be difficult, time-consuming, and costly. But when we look at self-care as a chance to honor God, our perspective starts to shift, and our work becomes more enjoyable. Sometimes exercise and moving our body can be like cheap therapy.

Not everyone views it the same way, so here are a few things that helped change my mind about taking care of the body God gave me:

- Pain is a part of the process. The pain of change and being proactive requires sacrifice, time, money, and discipline. The alternative is waiting until your health deteriorates and you're forced to make a change. The pain of waiting until later includes the same sacrifice, time, money, and discipline but on a much higher scale. You choose your pain.

- The time is now. Many people make excuses that the time isn't right. They'll say they're going to start on Monday, or January 1st, or when things calm down, but the truth is that there's never a right time. It's better to start on your own accord than to wait until you're forced to start because of health complications.

- Control what you can, accept what you can't. What we eat, how we move, and the way we rest is up to us. No one is stopping you but you. Take accountability for your choices and start doing it for Him.

Lord God, help me to honor You with my choices. Teach me to take accountability for my actions and to stop making excuses. Help me to be disciplined and dedicated with my health journey. I want to approach every task that's within my control with a passion and desire to glorify Your name. In Jesus' name, amen.

Amidst life's busyness, carve out a moment for honest reflection. What is the state of your self-care? In what areas do you need to improve? What are the steps you can take to begin that process? Invite a friend along with you on this journey for partnership and accountability.

44

SOWING AND REAPING

Remember this: Whoever sows sparingly will also reap sparingly, and whoever sows generously will also reap generously.

2 Corinthians 9:6

The measure to which we give is the measure to which we will receive. If you are tight-fisted and slow to help others, what you receive will be sparse and slow to arrive. Generosity isn't just a rule or a law, it's a lifestyle. It doesn't just apply to our finances, either. It includes our time, energy, effort, and resources.

Sowing is the act of planting a seed, while reaping is harvesting the produce of what you've planted. You have to sow before you can reap. Everyone is planting seeds through their choices, decisions, and actions that will one day grow into a harvest. Just as a farmer must first sow a seed, fertilize it, and then water it to reap a harvest, we, too, must sow seeds that please God so that our lives produce the good fruit of living like Christ. This is to be done out of love for God, love for one another, and love for our enemies.

Whatever we sow in life, we're going to reap, meaning that whatever we deposit is going to be returned to us. If we sow strong opinions or judgments, we're going to reap the same from other people. If we sow kindness, we're going to reap kindness. If we sow generosity, we will receive generosity. God set it up this way because He wants us to be more like Him. Practicing spiritual disciplines will help grow a great harvest of good in us that will please the Lord. Let this be a reminder to us to give generously of our time, energy, effort, and resources to those in need. You never know when you will be on the receiving end of someone else's generosity.

Lord, forgive me for holding back the things You've entrusted me with from people who need it. Show me how to live with faith, trusting that what I sow will return a harvest that reflects my heart. Teach me to steward my resources in a way that glorifies You. In Jesus' name, amen.

Make a list of acts of kindness that you are able to do. Get creative. Ask someone else or a small group to join your resources to bless someone else. Then go perform an act of kindness that reflects Christ's love.

45

HEAVENLY GUIDANCE

Trust in the LORD with all your heart and lean not on your own understanding; in all your ways submit to him, and he will make your paths straight.

Proverbs 3:5–6

I can't tell you all the different ways that leaning on my own understanding has gotten me in trouble. It never fails. I've found myself upside down in a ditch or lost in life's mountains with no cell service too many times. I make life harder for myself when I'm at the wheel. It's not from a lack of trying. I've just made poor judgment calls at times and couldn't see what God sees. Things that seemed right in my eyes were the very things that destroyed me, and I didn't use discernment.

Our understanding is temporary and limited, and it is driven by comfort and ease. God is looking at things through the scope of eternity—He is more concerned with our character development and the fulfillment of His will. Every day we must remind ourselves that His path is the best path even if it doesn't look like it. It would be helpful if the path God wants us on was just a straight path, but the path He laid out for us is scattered and inconsistent; however, it is in complete order. He puts us all on fragmented paths so that we must rely on His guidance because we don't know what lies ahead.

God sees the big picture while we see only what's right in front of us. Trusting the Lord with all our heart means that we'll have to make some hard choices. We'll have to say no when we want to say yes. We'll have to go places He calls us to even if those places look like a detour. But by submitting to a power that's greater than our own, we'll have the faith to go wherever and whenever He calls.

Father God, guide me by Your Spirit and lead me on the path You've laid out before me. I need You! The choices I make outside of Your plan lead me astray. I submit to Your lordship and leadership. Take me by the hand and illuminate the path You'd have me follow. I want what You want for me because I trust that You want what's best for me. In Jesus' name, amen.

How has leaning on your own understanding affected the path you are on right now? What is one hard choice that will help you get yourself back on His path fully? Write out Proverbs 3:5–6 and place it somewhere prominent.

46

NURTURING YOUR FAMILY

Your wife will be like a fruitful vine within your house; your children will be like olive shoots around your table.

Psalm 128:3

People often blame the government, the school system, the media, and everyone else for their family's development, but the reality is that responsibility lands on us. We can't trust others to instill values, godly character, and biblical teaching to the ones we love. It is our responsibility to lead and guide our families in the way they should go.

Even if you aren't a parent, God has placed people in your life who long for your guidance and support. He has given you the task and privilege of nurturing and helping them develop. This involves incorporating principles and values from your faith into your daily life.

The privilege of investing in people who look up to us, whether they're our spouse, children, or friends, comes with the responsibility of guiding them in the ways of the Lord. We can build them up, equip them, and send them out into the world to make an impact for Jesus. We need to hold ourselves accountable and instill the habits of prayer, Bible study, church attendance, service, and family worship. We must model virtuous behavior, teach values, foster open communication, set boundaries, encourage individual spiritual growth, and handle conflict with love.

When I stopped allowing the world to shape my family and started leading in a godly way, the change was significant. My family is far from perfect, but I can boldly say that when I started to step up to the plate, God moved in unimaginable ways within my family.

It takes intentionality to lead others. We can always improve, so this isn't an indictment or meant to make you feel guilty. My hope is that this stirs you to action to make some necessary adjustments and to become invested in the spiritual growth of those whom God has given you.

Lord God, *You have entrusted me with the spiritual development of those around me. Help me to be the leader You've called me to be. Teach me to be intentional with how I build up Your sons and daughters. Give me the insight and direction I need to steward well those who are in my sphere of influence. In Jesus' name, amen.*

How are you doing with leading the spiritual development of your family and loved ones? How can you grow in spiritually leading them? In what area do you most want to bear fruit? What tangible evidence do you see presently of your Christlike leadership, and what do you want to see in the future? Write these thoughts down in your journal.

47

THE TEST OF FAITH AND PATIENCE

We do not want you to become lazy, but to imitate those who through faith and patience inherit what has been promised.

Hebrews 6:12

Practicing patience can be a challenge. The world we live in operates at a rapid and dynamic pace. There are constant technological advancements, globalization, instant gratification, cultural expectations, and deadline-driven work. It's no wonder that when it comes to prayer, we get upset when things don't come in a timely manner or go according to our schedules.

On the other hand, we also tend to be lazy. The fact that we can get most things how and when we want means we don't have a strong work ethic. Our culture has become lethargic and complacent. We've lost our grit, consistency, and resolve. This isn't to say that the strides we've made are offset by the things we've lost, but it has hindered our spiritual lives.

Pioneers of our faith went through unimaginable trials and were tested in ways that would crush many of us today. We've become spiritually numb. We don't pray as though our lives depend on it. We don't search Scripture as if it is filled with truth. We don't gather with Christlike believers to sharpen our character. Those who've gone before us are examples for us to emulate so that we don't have to make the same mistakes.

Who do you resonate with in the Bible? Is it Abraham, a man who had his faith and patience tested? Maybe Peter, who was quick tempered, impulsive, and always putting his foot in his mouth? Could it be Joseph, someone who took bad situations and used them for the glory of God? Whoever it is, how can you learn from their wins and losses? How can their faith and patience encourage you in the season you're in?

> *Dear God, I've gotten lost in my comfort and have allowed my relationship with You to become stale. Revive my love, passion, and zeal for You and Your Word. Give me patience and faith for*

*the season I'm in. Help me to learn from those
who've gone before me, and teach me to seek
You in all things. In Jesus' name, amen.*

Think through the biblical men listed above. Which pioneer of faith did you resonate with? Why? Write down several ways that you can be more patient, less careless, and more intentional when it comes to your relationship with God.

48

TRAINING IN GODLINESS

For physical training is of some value, but godliness has value for all things, holding promise for both the present life and the life to come.

1 Timothy 4:8

Physical fitness is great, but it means nothing if your soul isn't healthy. When I was in the fitness industry, I helped people transform their bodies in ways they never thought imaginable. From college and professional athletes, high level bodybuilders and physique competitors, to my friendly neighbor down the street, I've led hundreds of clients in weight loss journeys and life transformations. It was a fulfilling career until I realized that

I was helping them achieve their physical goals but was leaving their spiritual lives empty.

I witnessed many of my clients achieving what they believed impossible only to realize they weren't happy or satisfied. There was something missing. You can be the most fit and in-shape person on the planet but still lack purpose if your spiritual and emotional health are neglected.

I sensed that God was saying it was time for a change. I had the desire to help people, but I became more interested in seeing their spiritual lives thrive. What I found is that when a spiritual life is grounded and healthy, the other aspects of life tend to follow suit. A healthy spiritual life leads to a strong emotional life, which should ultimately lead to a healthy physical life.

What I know to be true in the scope of eternity is that having a solid foundation of faith is far more important and urgent than being in shape. One thing I suggest is building a solid community of support in each category. Make sure you're around the right people that will call you higher spiritually, physically, and emotionally.

God, I don't want to give all my time, energy, effort, and resources to things that have no eternal significance. Teach me to steward my time and resources well. Help me identify what's important to You and reveal in me the areas that I need the most work. Search me, Lord, and help me be the best version of who You've called me to be. In Jesus' name, amen.

Which area—physically, spiritually, or emotionally—is your strongest? In which area do you need the most improvement? How can you focus on this area more? What action steps can you take to see improvement?

49

CONTENTMENT AND RICHES

Keep your lives free from the love of money and be content with what you have, because God has said, "Never will I leave you; never will I forsake you."

Hebrews 13:5

If you don't keep your life free from the love of money, God will. He has a way of dismissing anything that is in competition with Him. God will strike down the idols that we exalt. There was a time in my life when I was never content, and my life revolved around getting money. I would step on anyone in my way to get what I wanted. My god was money, and it was the only thing I was chasing. God didn't let that last too long.

When you love money more than God, you're willing to compromise your spiritual well-being to get it. My life was in shambles, and I didn't even realize it. I just knew I was never truly happy. I always felt empty. That's because money will never fulfill us. Only God can fulfill us.

It's scary how we can be so blind in the moment that we don't realize the depths of depravity in which we're operating. Thankfully, God allows our kingdoms to come crashing down so that we can realize we are made to serve His Kingdom. After falling into the trap of worldly success and failing, we need to learn the habit of constantly checking in with our heart, intentions, motives, and character so that we don't fall out of alignment with God's will for our life.

Your "why" and "for whom" must be rooted in God. Godly contentment should accompany your conviction, and there shouldn't be evidence that your love for money surpasses your love for Him.

Let this stir you to reflect on and examine your relationship to money, finances, success, and accomplishments. Don't forget whose you are and for whom you live. If you find that you're veering off track, make the necessary adjustments, seek godly counseling, employ some accountability, and implement some guardrails that keep you from flying off the rails.

Dear God, I know that You're always with me. Help me to keep You first. Forgive me for allowing things to replace You as the priority in my life. Teach me to seek Your face above all other things. Show me how to live a life that is characterized by commitment to You and contentment in my heart. In Jesus' name, amen.

Have you compromised your spiritual well-being to gain access to more money? Make a list of some of the guardrails you can put in place to keep your priorities in alignment with God's priorities for your life. Let someone you trust see your list so that you can be held accountable to them and select one item to implement today.

50

A FUTURE OF RESTORATION

"'He will wipe every tear from their eyes. There will be no more death' or mourning or crying or pain, for the old order of things has passed away."

Revelation 21:4

It can be hard to stay positive when we're bombarded with news of war, famine, disease, and natural disasters every day. It's a scary time to be alive. How are we to find hope and peace amid all the chaos? What are we supposed to hold on to?

The future promise of what's to come is where we can get our hope and peace. The Bible never says there will be world peace and an end to all suffering. We shouldn't wait for the world to come together, link arms, and sing

"Kumbaya." We should be looking to Jesus for the future promises He makes to us.

The restoration of the original design that God had for mankind will be reestablished. On that day, all the things that are heavy and burdensome will be no more. Our eyes can have hope in eternity. We can hold on to the picture of being embraced by the Lord of lords and the King of kings and having every tear wiped from our eyes.

We find our strength from knowing that the world we live in will pass away. There will be a new way of life. This doesn't mean that we throw our hands up in the air and quit. But it does remind us to continue forward, press on in our faith, and have a sense of urgency for the people in our sphere of influence to know Jesus.

Heavenly Father, help me to see the beauty of Your grand design. The thought of the end is too much for me to comprehend but I know You're good and faithful. Teach me to hold on to Your truth and to find comfort in Your loving promises. I look forward to the day that You wipe away every tear. In Jesus' name, amen.

How do the troubles you see in the world affect your thoughts and emotions? What are your coping strategies for dealing with this angst? How does the thought of entering eternity comfort you? As you think about these questions, journal your answers. Give your fears to Jesus, and picture Him wiping away each of your tears.

51

A LEGACY OF LOVE

But from everlasting to everlasting the Lord's love is with those who fear him, and his righteousness with their children's children—with those who keep his covenant and remember to obey his precepts.

Psalm 103:17–18

We all want to leave a lasting legacy. We want to be remembered and have our actions have an impact long after we're gone. I used to believe this meant leaving money, material possessions, and accomplishments to our children and loved ones. I've learned, however, that the spiritual legacy I leave behind is far more important than anything else I leave.

We want to leave a legacy of love for the Lord and a legacy of obedience to His Word. Being known for how we served Christ will last far longer than any amount of money. Taking care of your family is an important goal, of course, but it has less of an eternal impact.

Ponder this question: If today was your last day on earth, what would you be leaving behind? Is it a substantial amount of money and resources? Is it a life lived with love, purpose, and submission to God? Is it both or neither? Be someone who serves others, models unconditional love, makes sacrifices for the greater good, prioritizes relationships, lives a life of integrity, instills values, is a good listener, and follows the Lord with joy. Life is short, and we're not promised tomorrow. You might be reading this and think it's too late, but it's not. Start today. Ask your loved ones for forgiveness. Repent for the mistakes you've made. Make genuine changes. Be intentional about turning things around.

Maya Angelou once said, "I've learned that people will forget what you said, people will forget what you did, but people will never forget how you made them feel."* Start letting the people you love know how much you care today.

Father God, You have shown us how to love. Help me to love without borders, to serve without

*Dr. Maya Angelou, "I've Learned That People Will Forget What You Said . . ." *Oprah.com*, 2024, https://www.oprah.com/quote/quote-about -making-a-difference-maya-angelou.

counting the cost, and to care deeply about the things that move Your heart. Teach me to be more concerned with heavenly things than earthly entanglements. May I leave a legacy of love and obedience to Your Word. In Jesus' name, amen.

Write down the legacy of love that you want to leave behind. What is something you can do today to build that legacy and let someone know how much you care?

52

ROOTED AND BUILT UP IN FAITH

So then, just as you received Christ Jesus as Lord,
continue to live your lives in him, rooted and built up
in him, strengthened in the faith as you were taught,
and overflowing with thankfulness.

Colossians 2:6–7

Our lives in Christ don't make sense to those who aren't believers. The way we respond to the problems of life looks different. We have a hope, a strength, and a faith that will confuse anyone who doesn't know Jesus. Or at least we should.

When we are rooted and built up in Him, joy and thankfulness pour out of us regardless of our circumstances. We can have a smile on our face in the middle of a storm because we're not clinging to the hope of a life immune to trials. Instead, we're holding on to the hope of eternity. That's what anchors and roots us.

Too many times we allow what we're going through to become our life's odometer. When things are good and the seas are calm, we think God is good and pleased with us. When the waves get choppy and the wind starts to blow, we immediately start wondering what we did wrong and if God's mad at us. That's a worldly mentality, and as believers, we should be thinking differently.

We must not allow our circumstances to dictate what we believe about the character of God. Get off the rollercoaster of emotions that's your life and stand on the solid foundation of truth that is found in Jesus.

When you recognize that you're letting your mind get the best of you, take it to God. Prayer works great, but I also love to run to the Bible. In whatever situation you find yourself, ask what the Bible says about it. No matter what you're going through, you'll always be encouraged by the truth about God's character, His nature, or your identity as a believer, which will bring you comfort and peace.

Father God, thank You for giving me hope and being a constant source of strength. Teach me to stay rooted in You and to allow Your Word to be my comfort and peace. Help me to remember that I can't do things on my own and that when I feel overwhelmed, I need to run to You. In Jesus' name, amen.

When has your life been marked by joy and thankfulness, even during storms? What is one step you can take to ensure that you don't allow the circumstances around you to dictate your trust in the Lord?

53

HANDLING STRESS

Cast your cares on the LORD and he will sustain you;
he will never let the righteous be shaken.

Psalm 55:22

Stress is an inevitable part of life. It comes in many forms—work, family, health, finances, life transitions, and our environment. While we may not have control over the situations that trigger stress, we do have control over how we respond to it. I work with a ton of people in ministry, which comes with instability and stress because people are sporadic and unpredictable. I can't say that I've always responded to stress in a positive manner, but I can say that since I started being intentional about my reactions, I became more effective.

Here are a few strategies I use to handle my stress:

- Prayer and devotion to start the day. When we take time at the beginning of the day to fill our cup with the things of God, no matter how hard we're squeezed, only things of God pour out of us.

- Healthy nutrition and exercise choices. When we're stressed, we feel out of control. When we nurture our physical and mental health, we're able to handle things that are out of our control much better.

- Take breaks. Be sure to take small breaks to stretch, breathe, walk, clear your mind, and pray. Sometimes we sit in stress longer than needed, and a quick unplug helps to reboot our brains and get refocused.

- Journal. Make time in the morning or at the end of the day to take the thoughts, worries, and cares swirling in your mind and pour them out on paper. This practice helps to make space in our mind and helps us organize our thoughts. One thing that stresses me out is forgetting things that are important, so putting them on paper relieves that stress immediately.

Recognize the specific factors causing you stress so that you can address them more effectively with God. Implement faith-based coping strategies that work best for you and be consistent with them. Do not allow stress to turn you away from your faith.

> *Heavenly Father,* I lay all my cares, worries, and burdens down at the foot of Your throne. I surrender all the things that cause me stress. Give me a peace that transcends all understanding and help me manage the things I can control in an honorable way. Teach me to accept the things I cannot change and help me to trust You. In Jesus' name, amen.

How do you handle life's stresses? What faith-based strategies can you add to that list? Write a couple of those on sticky notes and place them around your house to read when a stressful situation arises.

54

TREASURES IN HEAVEN

"Do not store up for yourselves treasures on earth, where moths and vermin destroy, and where thieves break in and steal. But store up for yourselves treasures in heaven, where moths and vermin do not destroy, and where thieves do not break in and steal. For where your treasure is, there your heart will be also."

Matthew 6:19–21

One of my all-time favorite sayings is, "You won't ever see a hearse with a U-Haul attached to the back." It's a great reminder that you can't take any of your stuff with you when you die. Money, material belongings, awards; it all gets left behind. I can't tell you how many times I've spoken to older folks who say they regret never serving out their true purpose in life because they were consumed and devoted to accumulating things. Ultimately, things don't matter.

It isn't bad or evil to have nice things, live well, travel widely, or wear nice clothes. But that shouldn't be the sole focus of our existence. Those things expire, rot, deteriorate, are destroyed, and fall apart. We are called to live for eternity and heavenly things.

The world tries to convince us that life is all about storing up stuff. It paints a picture of success being someone who has the best things life has to offer. This lie is powerful, and people are still falling for it. The belief that satisfaction comes from accumulating more has a stronghold on this generation and the minds of the masses.

The truth is that even the most powerful and rich people who live luxurious lifestyles aren't necessarily happy. They take their own lives at an alarmingly high rate. They change spouses like they change wardrobes. They're addicted to drugs, alcohol, and sex. If money, materials, and power brought happiness, people would be happy—but they're not. This world only provides empty promises. If you don't have Jesus, you will never truly be happy and fulfilled. The true treasure is an eternal life in heaven.

Father, I know that I can't take any of these things with me when I come home to You. Help me love

You more than the things I've been chasing after. Solidify this commitment in my heart and help me let go of worldly pursuits to follow You. This world only provides empty promises, so teach me how to put my faith in You. In Jesus' name, amen.

How are your finances, resources, and treasures currently invested? Which kingdom do you think they are building more: yours or God's? What is one investment you can make today that will last eternally?

55

WALKING WITH CONFIDENCE

Even though I walk through the darkest valley, I will fear no evil, for you are with me; your rod and your staff, they comfort me.

Psalm 23:4

There is a boldness and confidence that we can have as followers of Jesus because of the God we serve. No matter what we're going through or dealing with, we have all we need because we have Jesus. While this sounds fanatical and crazy to the world, followers of Jesus walk with confidence even during hard moments because we know the truth, and the truth sets us free. We do not fear evil because we have our Protector. It may take us some time to gain that confidence in the midst of adversity, but nonetheless, we do find it.

One of the greatest tools the enemy uses against us is distraction. He distracts us from the truth. He distracts us from God's voice. He distracts us with his obstacles and our issues. He tries to get us to focus on the problem rather than on God. The enemy gets loud, puffs himself up, and tries to appear more powerful than he really is. Like the wizard in *The Wizard of Oz*, he hides behind smoke screens, a loud voice, and a curtain of lies. When we pull the curtain back and expose him with the truth of the Word of God, he flees because he has no authority over our soul. He runs and hides because the power in us is greater than the power in this world.

No matter what valley you're in or evil you're surrounded by, know that God is with you. He hasn't left you. He's right there in the thick of things with you. Don't be discouraged that He hasn't removed you from the problem. Many times, it's in the middle of those problems that He's developing you and preparing you for things to come. You don't want to miss out on crucial character development because you are a little uncomfortable. Be courageous.

God, thank You for never leaving me. Help me to see Your hand even when I don't feel it. Teach me to walk in confidence and courage knowing that You are always with me. Show me how to fight battles in Your strength and not my own. Equip me with the boldness to go where You call and to move without hesitation. I pray all this in the power of Jesus' name, amen.

Ask God to show you the practices, possessions, habits, or relationships that have distracted you from Him. What tricks has the devil used to distract you? What can you do differently when distractions come?

56

YOUR FAMILY'S IDENTITY

See what great love the Father has lavished on us,
that we should be called children of God! And that is
what we are!

1 John 3:1

aving a healthy sense of who you are as a family is paramount. Family identity is a shared sense of belonging, values, beliefs, traditions, and characteristics that define a particular family unit. It is what distinguishes your family from others and what creates a sense of cohesion and connection within your family.

What is the foundation of your family's identity? It should be anchored in the fact that we are children of God. That truth should be what holds us together and defines our traditions, shapes our decisions, and guides our choices.

The enemy's goal is to attack families by trying to confuse their identity and redefine the truth of who each individual is. This is why we have to build on solid ground—the Word of God. What better rock to build on than Jesus? The enemy is coming for the children in your life, and it's your responsibility to build them up in their identity so that no matter what they come up against, they know who they are in Christ.

You can shape the identity and set the tone for your family. What's important to you will be important to them. They may not have the same passion and hunger for God, but how you lead and live plants seeds that will sprout when the time is right. Identity isn't something that's taught, it is caught. How consistent is your prayer life? How often do you read the Bible or have a regular devotional time? How is your attitude and reactions to trials? Do you gossip about people more than you pray for them? These things matter.

Everything you do should stem from the immutable truth that you are a child of God. When you set the tone by living it out, your family is bound to catch on. Reflect on areas in your life where you can make improvements and adjustments.

Lord God, You have given me new life. Help me to live in a way that glorifies You. I pray that my family and those who are close to me understand their identity as Your children. Teach me to be a model of that truth and a reminder to those who might have forgotten. May You be glorified. In Jesus' name, amen.

What is one step you can take today to ground or re-ground yourself in your identity as a child of God?

57

THE AUTHOR AND FINISHER OF OUR FAITH

Fixing our eyes on Jesus, the pioneer and perfecter of faith. For the joy set before him he endured the cross, scorning its shame, and sat down at the right hand of the throne of God.

Hebrews 12:2

There's a saying in the sports world that you should keep your eye on the prize. When shooting a free throw in basketball, you should shoot the ball at the back of the rim for an accurate shot. When running, you should focus on a destination point ahead and, once you've reached it, focus on a new destination point until you have completed your goal. In archery, you are to fix your eyes on the bullseye to increase your accuracy. What you set your eyes on matters.

What are you fixing your eyes on? Is it your past, with all your mistakes and failures? Or is your gaze fixed on a future that is filled with fear of the unknown, worry, and angst? As Christians, we need to have our eyes fixed on Jesus. He showed us how to keep our eyes on the prize even during challenging circumstances. As He neared the end of His life and was about to face the cross on our behalf, He understood that the purpose of the moment was greater than His pain and discomfort.

As believers, we can live like that. We can see that our temporary discomfort and pain is small when compared to eternity. When we are heavenly minded and our eyes are fixed on Jesus, we can endure anything that life throws at us.

When we are faced with tough times, we have a choice. Do we look at the situation through the lens of our limitations, or do we look at it through the lens of our Lord? How would Jesus respond? Would He complain, feel sorry for Himself, and throw in the towel? Or would He understand that His life has a greater meaning, that God has a plan, and that He is in full control? Life can be hard, but we can find strength when we're focused on Him.

Lord God, remind me to keep my eyes fixed on You. When life knocks me down, help me to remember that You're always with me and You'll never leave me. You are my strength. Teach me to rely on You and never to forget that You're in control. My joy comes from knowing You. In Jesus' name, amen.

What do your eyes drift to when you're faced with disappointment or pain? Write out a helpful Bible verse and place it in prominent places for you to reflect upon.

58

BALANCING WELLNESS

*Dear friend, I pray that you may enjoy good health
and that all may go well with you, even as your soul
is getting along well.*

3 John 1:2

There are several dimensions of wellness. These include, but aren't limited to, your physical, mental, emotional, and spiritual well-being. Each plays a vital part in your overall health. They shouldn't be neglected because they're interconnected. The unfortunate truth is that most of us are out of balance. You may excel in one area, but chances are you need some work in another.

When I was in the fitness industry, I could boast that I was in the best shape of my life, but emotionally and spiritually I was bankrupt. It took some humbling circumstances for me to realize this. When I started working on improving those other areas, my physical fitness took a hit. I started to focus heavily on my spiritual and emotional wellness, and that put my physical health on the back burner.

It's a balancing act. There's a sweet spot we must find where we take the time, energy, effort, and resources to invest into each dimension in a way that doesn't completely rob the others. This is a lifelong journey that involves making conscious choices and adopting healthy habits that align with your personal values and goals. Regular self-assessment and adjustments to your lifestyle can help you achieve and maintain wellness, leading to a higher quality of life and a greater sense of fulfillment.

As you're reading this, what areas of your life seem out of balance? Is there an area that needs more work than the others? Maybe you feel like it's all of them. Use this day's challenge to stir your mind and shed light on a few opportunities for growth.

Start out with gradual and sustainable changes and improvements. List the areas that you do well in and see if there are ways to add in an element that will benefit another area. If you excel in physical wellness, for instance, listen to a spiritual podcast or sermon while working out. Maybe journal after each workout as you cool down to check in with your mental health. Small steps in the right direction will lead to an overall balanced wellness.

Father God, help me not to neglect my overall well-being. Help me to check in regularly in all aspects of life and reveal to me the areas where I may be lacking. Guide me in spirit and truth and show me how to live a healthful life for Your honor and glory. In Jesus' name, amen.

In an area of wellness that needs improvement, what is one sustainable change you can begin to make today to see growth?

59

TRUE RICHES

A good name is more desirable than great riches; to be esteemed is better than silver or gold.

Proverbs 22:1

Life is short. We are here today and gone tomorrow. What we leave behind is important. Leaving a legacy of righteous living is far greater than anything else, and it's the truest form of wealth. Your desire should be to leave behind a name that will forever be associated with love, service, selflessness, and integrity. A lasting legacy is the positive impact your life has on other people.

While this world obsesses over wealth and riches, God wants you to have a wealth of love and a willingness to put others first. He wants you to live a life that has an impact on people's lives. He wants you to be known for being faithful to His Word, and He wants you to be rich in your faith. He wants you to demonstrate your faith through your actions and daily life and treat others with kindness, compassion, and integrity. He wants you to be consistent in your values at work, in your community, and at home, and to engage in acts of service and charity. He wants you to connect with people on a personal level, to avoid flaunting wealth and material possessions, and to make choices that align with your faith and values.

We can find ourselves more wrapped up in leaving a financial legacy than investing in a spiritual one. Remember that a legacy of loving the Lord and following Him obediently is priceless. Passing down a life lived with character is more important than modeling a life lived with comfort.

> *Lord, help me to live a life of impact that touches people's lives for Your glory. Teach me to use what I've been given to honor You and to serve those in my sphere of influence. Show me how to leave a legacy of faithfulness to Your Word and to make a good name that is worth more than great riches. In Jesus' name, amen.*

What do you want to be remembered for? From the things listed above that God wants you to be known for, select one and commit to implementing that trait into your routine.

60

A HOPE THAT ANCHORS THE SOUL

We have this hope as an anchor for the soul, firm and secure.

Hebrews 6:19

What is your anchor? What's holding you steady when the waves of life beat against your boat? Life's journey is often filled with unpredictable seas, unbearable waves, and unforeseen storms. Just as a ship relies on a steadfast anchor to remain grounded during turbulent times, our souls find stability in the hope we have in God's promises.

Anchoring our souls is the firm and secure hope that God will always sustain us and never let us down. This is not a fleeting optimism or wishful thinking that changes the winds of our circumstances. It is a deep, abiding confidence in the faithfulness of God.

Imagine an anchor dropping into the depths of the sea, reaching down to a solid foundation, and locking itself into the seabed. The ship attached to that anchor will no longer drift away. In the same way, our hope in God reaches into the depths of our soul and provides a secure foundation amid the uncertainties of life. As we go through challenges, let us anchor our souls in the unchanging character of our Creator.

Let's remember that our anchor holds a lot of power. It keeps our vessel in place even when subjected to external forces. A well-set anchor provides sufficient resistance to those forces. If you put your hope in awards, achievements, finances, family, and health, don't be surprised when none of them hold you steady or secure when times get hard.

May the hope that anchors your soul bring peace in the storms, assurance in uncertainty, and comfort in times of turmoil. It's a lifeline holding you steady at all times. Having a clear sense of God's purpose and meaning for your life will serve as the ultimate anchor for your soul.

Lord God, my hope is You and in You alone. Take away anything that tries to compete for first place in my heart. Be the anchor to my soul, and don't allow me to drift away. Search my heart and teach me to reflect often. You are my firm foundation, my place of refuge and security. Comfort me in Your loving embrace. In Jesus' name, amen.

What do you rely on to keep you steady when you face life's difficulties? If that anchor is anything but Jesus, ask Him for forgiveness and if He would anchor your soul in His unchanging character.

ANDREW F CARTER is the founder and lead pastor of Royal City Church. Andrew also travels as a guest speaker at churches, events, conferences, and retreats. He is known for his testimony, appearing on television networks, podcasts, and stages preaching the Good News of Jesus Christ. Andrew creates influential social media content for his millions of followers. He is a pastor, author, husband, and father. To learn more about Andrew, visit www.AndrewFCarter.com. You can also find Andrew on all major social media platforms @AndrewFCarter.